Wild Birds

Designs for Appliqué & Quilting

CAROL ARMSTRONG

 C&T PUBLISHING

© Copyright 2000 Carol Armstrong

Developmental Editor: Barbara Konzak Kuhn

Technical Editor: Sara Kate MacFarland

Cover Design: Kristen Yenche

Back cover photo: *Feathered Stars* Cover photo: Detail of *Hummingbirds and Fuchsia*

Book Design: Kristen Yenche

Illustrator: Norman Remer © C&T Publishing

Photography: Sharon Risedorph

Attention Teachers: C&T Publishing, Inc. encourages you to use this book as a text for teaching. Contact us at 800-284-1114 or www.ctpub.com for more information about the C&T Teachers Program.

Library of Congress Cataloging-in-Publication Data

Armstrong, Carol,
Wild birds : designs for appliqué & quilting / Carol Armstrong.
p. cm.
Includes bibliographical references and index.
ISBN 1-57120-087-8 (paper trade)
1. Appliqué--Patterns. 2. Quilting--Patterns. 3. Birds in art. I. Title.
TT779 .A76 2000
746.44'5041--dc21

99-006920
CIP

Published by C&T Publishing, Inc.
P.O. Box 1456
Lafayette, California 94549

Printed in China

10 9 8 7 6 5 4 3 2 1

Table of Contents

Introduction

Birds. They brighten our world with their beautiful color, their sparkling song, and their wonderful gift of flight. We love watching them at our feeders throughout the year. We love seeking them out in their natural habitat. Here, I have captured images of our feathered friends in appliqué and quilting for you to enjoy.

As you proceed, abandon templates and adopt a lightbox to learn my style of appliqué. Add dimension to your birds by using more feathers rather than solid patches of color. Shades of color plus the shadows formed by the appliqué combine and bring life to these fabric birds. A bit of branch, a juicy berry, or a leafy sprig puts each bird in its own world.

Adding to the colorful appliquéd pictures are wonderful shades and textures created by quilting patterns, which fill the background. Learn my no-mark quilting techniques to add rain, wind, feathers, or pebbles within nature's random design. Enjoy the surprises that may arise as you create your own combination of shapes and lines.

As you observe birds, also note the patterns of branches on the trees, the pebbles of the stream bank, or a patch of swaying cattails. All that nature creates is inspiration for quilting designs.

To those new to appliqué, my relaxed technique makes learning fun. For those who are experienced in appliqué, my design techniques will increase your possibilities. To all, I hope appliqué and quilting give you the same joy I gain as I sew.

To Ann, thank you.

CHAPTER ONE

Supplies

Following is a list of supplies that you will need for hand appliqué and quilting. If you use quality materials, your time investment will be well worth the effort. Happy Appliqué!

NEEDLES

Small needles make finer stitches. My choice for appliqué is a #10 milliners by Richard Hemming & Son. The extra length gives more control when needle-turning the edges on the small appliqué pieces. I use a #10 sharps for quilting but you may also want to try a betweens needle, which is shorter. You will need a larger-eyed embroidery needle for embroidering details.

THIMBLES

You will have happier fingers if you use a thimble to keep them puncture free. I use a small leather thimble on my needle-pushing finger when quilting. But on the back of the quilt I like to feel the needle and find that it keeps my stitches even. There are many styles of thimbles and quilting aids. I tried several until I chose the one that works best for me.

CUTTING TOOLS

It is important to have good sharp scissors. You will need a small pair for snipping threads and clipping curves. A larger pair will serve for cutting fabrics. Both sizes should cut to the tip of the blades. A rotary cutter, mat, and ruler are invaluable for squaring up and for cutting borders and bindings.

LIGHTBOX

A lightbox is essential for appliquéing without templates. It makes tracing and marking designs quick and easy. Art supply stores, as well as many quilt and craft shops, carry lightboxes in a variety of sizes. In lieu of a lightbox, a window on a sunny day or a glass table with a small lamp underneath will serve you well.

PINS

I always have a number of glass-head and regular fine pins on hand. (Always discard any pin with a burr, nick, or bend; these may pull a thread in your work.) Pins are helpful when positioning appliqué pieces and sewing on borders and bindings.

MARKING IMPLEMENTS

A good selection of marking pens and pencils is a must for appliqué and quilting. There are many to choose from at your quilt shop. It is essential to test any marker to see if the ink or lead is removable. My best markers are a white pencil and a silver pencil such as Verithin™. I use whichever one shows the best on the color of fabric. The disappearing or washout pens work well for marking quilting lines when necessary, but test them first. I use them sparingly. Never iron a marked piece of fabric; remove the marking first. The best advice is to always mark lightly.

LIGHTING

Work in a well-lit area to make sewing easier and more relaxing. I prefer stitching in daylight, with a lamp for appliqué, especially when working with darker fabrics or two overlapping pieces of the same color. Evening sewing requires a good light source to be enjoyable.

IRON

A clean steam iron is a basic sewing aid. I iron on a padded surface. (A few white towels on an ironing or pressing board works well.) Set the iron on a cotton setting and use some steam. Press appliquéd pieces from the back. Do not hold the iron in one place too long or overheat the fabric, or some fabric dyes may melt and move. Gently press the appliqué piece flat. The padded surface helps to keep the appliqué smooth.

GETTING COMFORTABLE

Finding a comfortable place to sew is important. When appliquéing, either raising one knee or placing a pillow on your lap is helpful in controlling the background fabric. Using a footstool helps elevate your knee and prevents you from bending forward and tensing as you sew. Try to keep your hands in a straight position with little wrist bending. You will know when you have found the position that works best for you when you have sewn for several hours and you are as relaxed as when you began. However, you should always get up and move around once an hour. (This at least will let you get some of your chores done.)

FABRIC

I recommend using 100% cotton fabric because it is the easiest to handle for appliqué. Pure cotton will happily respond to a finger-press, staying in place as you work. For my birds, flowers, and trees, I use only solid or almost-solid colors. Birds require many shades of browns, grays, and blacks, so I am always looking for different shades of these basic colors for my stash. In the same way, shades of green for the growing world are needed and the rest of the rainbow for all other needs. The muslin I use is pre-shrunk, unbleached, and perma-pressed. I use the grain of the fabric when it is helpful, but most often I ignore it.

Pre-wash your fabrics if you plan on washing the finished piece. Always test for colorfastness by soaking the fabric in cool water until the water is clear. Or iron a small wet piece on a white fabric to see if the color moves. If after all rinsing the color continues to run, do not use that piece. You may pre-shrink all your fabrics in the dryer, but remove the pieces while they are still damp and finish drying them by pressing them with an iron set on cotton.

BATTING

The majority of my wallhangings use Poly-fil Traditional™, a needle-punched batting. It has a blanket-like quality and gives excellent dimension, even when closely quilted. When I want an old-fashioned look or a thinner finished piece, I use one of the cotton battings available. These battings are nice for clothing or small quilted items.

THREAD

Use a thread quality that your fabric deserves. I quilt most often with a natural color thread on the unbleached muslin. I use 100% cotton or cotton-wrapped polyester thread for basting, appliquéing, and quilting. A white thread is best for basting. For quilting, a thread designed specifically for quilting is important. When appliquéing, match as closely as possible the color of the thread and the appliqué fabric. The closer the match, the more likely the stitches will seem to disappear. For best results, check the color match in natural light.

CHAPTER TWO

Lightbox Appliqué—
The Method

To eliminate tedious templates, I use a lightbox. This simplifies the process. Because my birds are composed of many different pieces, this method is especially welcome. The fewer the steps in creating your piece, the more fun you will have. Begin with a small project if you are new to appliqué.

GENERAL INSTRUCTIONS FOR LIGHTBOX APPLIQUÉ

Begin by drawing your design on a sheet of white paper with a medium-point black marker. Secure the pattern to the lightbox with masking tape.

Cut the background fabric at least one inch larger all around than needed. Appliqué may draw the fabric a bit. (You can trim the piece to the size needed after the appliqué is finished and the piece is pressed.) Lay the background fabric, right-side up on the lightbox, over the pattern. Using a water-soluble marker or a silver, white, or mechanical pencil, trace the entire design for appliqué onto the background fabric. Mark lightly so that any marks left showing after the appliqué is finished can be removed. Remove the background fabric from the lightbox, but leave the pattern in place.

Using the pattern taped to the lightbox, trace individual pieces onto the right side of the selected appliqué fabric with a white or silver pencil. Refer to the photographs and drawings throughout the book for color ideas. Trace the exact size of each piece as it is drawn on the design. This line will be your guide for turning under. Cut out each piece 3/16 to 1/4 inch larger than the marked line. After you are comfortable with the turn-under allowance, you can cut these by eye; then trim the excess fabric if necessary.

Indicate on the turn-under allowance of each piece its number for placement. This will help identify each piece, since many feathers and leaves are similar. While you are learning to appliqué, mark each piece, as well as the background, and always leave ample fabric to turn under. The extra fabric can always be trimmed away as necessary, and the larger initial piece is easier to work. As you gain experience, you may cut some little pieces free-hand and mark the background only (best when there are few overlapping pieces that require careful placement). Exact placement is often not necessary, as with leaves, berries, and branches.

When appliquéing with light-colored fabrics, add a lining of the same color fabric you are using to prevent the turn-under allowance from showing through. Cut a piece the exact size of the appliqué piece with no turn-under allowance and place it behind the piece to appliqué. Add a piece of batting for more dimension or to prevent shadowing.

Begin to stitch by using the numbers on the pattern for appliqué order. Pieces that are covered by another are sewn down first. Only turn under and sew those edges that are exposed, not those that will be covered by another piece. The lines on the background fabric guide the placement of each piece. Turn under the allowance to the line on the appliqué piece, using the needle as you stitch and matching it with the motif lines marked on the background fabric.

Appliqué order

Check often that the piece is lining up. Use a pin to hold the piece in place, if needed. Turn under enough fabric for only a few stitches: do not worry ten stitches ahead. The removable nature of the markings allows a plus-or-minus match, so relax as you stitch. A feather can be ruffled, the tip of a leaf can be nipped, or a bite can be taken from a berry. Close is good.

After the appliqué is finished, embroider the details such as the beak, eye, or feet. Remove any markings that show, and press the appliquéd piece from the back with a medium iron on a padded ironing surface. Trim the background to the required size.

ORDER OF APPLIQUÉ

Simply said, the pieces that are furthest away in the drawing are started first. That is, sew the pieces covered by any others first. Experience will make these decisions easier. I have marked the appliqué order for all the bird patterns. Pieces not numbered, such as leaves or berries, can be appliquéd at any time in the sequence. When appliquéing a motif that has a number of pieces which overlap, add a little extra allowance. This will help if there is any shifting as you sew. Excess fabric is there if things do not line up—and can be trimmed away if everything does line up. Do not hesitate to increase or decrease the length or width of the bird's feathers if needed. Fabric moves where you push it; just keep the work flat as you manipulate the pieces.

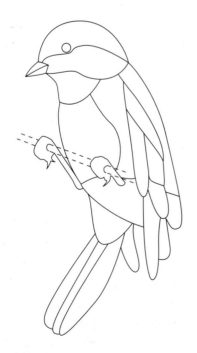

Completed chickadee

APPLIQUÉD APPLIQUÉ OR PRE-APPLIQUÉ APPROACH

This method is a welcome addition to any appliqué technique.

The method improves the look of many designs and makes positioning easier, especially on pre-made items. With basic appliqué, each piece is stitched to the background one at a time. With pre-appliqué, several or all pieces of a motif are stitched together before being stitched to the background. Pre-appliqué creates a smoother line along the motif edges where different pieces meet.

Basic guidelines for this technique are the same. Same stitch, same marking; the order of appliqué is similar. Appliqué each piece to the next, referring to the pattern. Do not stitch into the turn-under allowances; rather, leave them free. This makes it easier when sewing the motif to the background. Change the thread color to match the fabric you are sewing. Using a pincushion with pre-threaded needles in all the colors of the design is a great help. When the section or the entire motif is sewn together, stitch it to your background. Often you will sew several groups of pieces together and then sew them to each other. This is especially true with each of the birds.

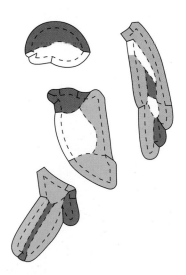

Pre-appliqué of chickadee

Note in the example that the tail, head, and body are assembled separately and then sewn together to make one unit. Using this method provides for accurate placement. Try not to stretch any pieces, and check frequently against the pattern. As you become more experienced in appliqué you will notice when this method is most effective. You will also become more adept at manipulating the fabric to do what you want and to go where you want.

THE APPLIQUÉ STITCH

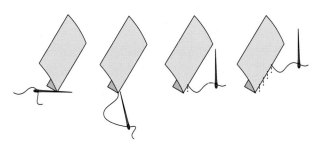

The appliqué stitch

Cut, knot, and thread the needle with a 12-inch to 18-inch single strand of thread in a color to match the fabric you are appliquéing. A very long thread will wear out before you use its entire length. Using the shaft of your needle, turn under the edge of the piece to the marked line. Slip the knot into the fold of the appliqué piece and out onto the edge to be stitched down. The knot will be hidden in the fold. This is especially nice if you are appliquéing pieces where the back will not be covered. It is helpful to keep the background reasonably taut when needle turning appliqué pieces. As you needle-turn, this prevents the needle from pushing the background along with the appliqué piece. I normally have the background fabric over my knee and the friction of fabric on fabric is enough to hold the unit. However, if it is a small background piece that you are working or if you are appliquéing near an edge, it is helpful to pin the background down in one spot. I pin it to my jeans or to a pillow on my lap. Since it is best to turn the piece as you sew, you should re-pin as you go. This "extra hand" keeps your work flat and gives you better results.

While holding the piece to be appliquéd in the desired place on the background, insert the needle into the background evenly with the thread's exit from the appliqué piece.

Move the needle tip forward with the needle still under the background, and then come up through background, catching a few threads on the folded edge of the appliqué piece. Pull the thread snugly without drawing up the fabric.

Again, insert the needle into the background even with the thread's last exit from the turned edge. Travel a bit under the background and come up through the background, catching a few threads on the folded edge. The stitches will appear directly on the fold. Keep folding the turn-under allowance with the shaft of the needle as you stitch; trim as necessary.

To keep your stitching consistent and comfortable, turn your work as you proceed. Only worry about the stitch at hand and not what is ahead, other than an occasional check to see if the piece will line up at the end when you get there. Try to begin your appliqué at an end point so that you sew the piece to the background in one continuous line. Remember to let yourself relax and create beautiful appliqué; do not fret over little differences. Nature varies everything, and so can you.

To end, secure the thread with three stitches in the same place. If there will be another piece covering the area, you can take these stitches on the right side. Otherwise, go to the back and take the stitches through the background fabric only, behind the appliqué, or tie a knot on the back if you prefer.

Being comfortable with the stitch is the key to appliqué. Practice is how to achieve this comfort. Try to keep your stitches small and evenly spaced. As you practice your appliqué, your stitches will become tiny, even, and automatic. Be as happy with your beginning pieces as your later ones as they are part of the adventure of learning.

INSIDE POINTS

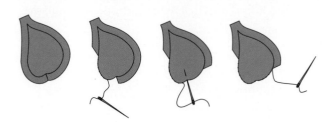

Inside point

Whenever possible I design my motifs to avoid inside points, but there are some shapes that need those inside points.

Clip to the inside point just shy of the marked turn-under line. Start stitching the piece at a comfortable place that will give you a continuous line of stitching, but not at the inside point. Stitch almost to the inside point, but turn under all the way to the clip.

With the needle, turn under part of the allowance, on the opposite side, down to the clip.
Hold in place.

Put the needle under the appliqué and pivot, rolling the allowance under and around the point. Hold in place and stitch to the inside point. Take one or more tiny stitches at the inside point, then adjust the turn-under on the way out of the inside point and continue around the piece.

If an inside point just won't work for you, cut the piece into two pieces and pre-appliqué the two together. Mark the line splitting the inside point. Cut two pieces with turn-under allowance, then pre-appliqué along the centerline. Appliqué as a single piece.

INSIDE CURVES

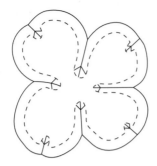

Clipping inside curve; dogwood blossom

For inside curves, clip as many times as needed for a smooth turn-under. When curves are tight, use the same pivoting needle method as used for inside points. Practice sewing tight curves and inside points on scrap fabric. My designs are created with as few difficult turning areas as possible.

POINTS

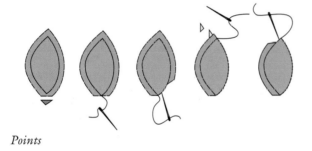

Points

Some shapes are easier to stitch when starting at a point: for example, the point of a leaf stem, the point of a tear-drop shape or a heart shape, a point at the center of a flower, or any piece where I will begin and end at the same point. Points are not difficult once you sew a few. The sharper the point, the slower you should work to ease the allowance under.

Square off the end of the point leaving 3/16-inch turn-under allowance. The best rule to follow is, if it is too much to turn under, cut it off. Fold under the allowance straight across the point. Bring your thread up through the exact point, hiding the knot in the fold. Take one stitch.

Hold the end down and using the shaft of the needle, turn under a portion of the allowance beyond the point, then stitch. Continue stitching to the next point. Make a stitch at the exact point on your appliqué shape. Take another very tiny second stitch to secure the piece. Clip the excess fabric at the point. Push the allowance under with your needle and start to stitch the second point.

You have now finished two points—one a beginning point and the other a point within a line of stitching. Not so bad, is it?

BIAS STRIPS

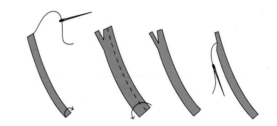

Bias stems

Use bias strips for stems, branches, or any thin line (See Branches, page 12) you want to appliqué, especially if the line is curved. Bias is cut at a 45° angle to the straight grain, is not easily frayed, and has some stretch.

For stitching larger widths of bias, simply cut your bias strip the width of the finished line plus the turn-under allowance on both sides. For example, cut a bias strip 3/4-inch wide for a desired 1/4-inch wide finished stem. Fingerpress one side and stitch in place following the marking on the background. Turn the other side under with your needle as you go. On a curve I sew the inside of the curve first.

For tiny bias, for little stems or vines, I cut the strip about 1/2-inch wide so that it is easier to handle. As with wider strips, fingerpress one side and stitch in place according to your design. Then flip the piece open to expose the turn-under allowance. Carefully trim it close to the stitched line, leaving enough fabric to secure the piece. Flip the piece back and trim to the width needed plus a $3/16$ inch or less turn-under. A good rule of thumb is to trim the turn-under allowance to the width of the finished stem. Needle-turn the allowance along the other side. You will be amazed at how tiny a line you can create with just a little practice.

CIRCLES

Circles

The circle is important in bird quilts, as birds go with berries and berries are round. But do not worry if there is a bite in your berry or that it looks a little stepped on. Remember the bird did it.

The best tip for turning circles, both large and small, is to take one stitch at a time and then turn. Again take one stitch and turn. If you end up with a little point along the curve, bring your needle out through the point and then back through the background, pulling the point inward. Use the marking on the background and the curve on the marked shape to assist in smooth lines.

FEATHERS

When cutting out feathers the grain of the fabric can affect your appliqué. If you cut the feather with the length along the grain you have a stable feather that is less likely to stretch, however it will ravel more easily as you sew. If you cut the feather with its length running along the bias, you have minimal raveling problems; however, be careful not to stretch it as you appliqué. Too much stretch will make the feather warp and will make the placement of overlapping feathers change.

Which to use? I vary according to fabrics. A slightly coarser cotton is best cut on the bias, using a few extra pins to hold the piece as you appliqué. On tighter-weave cottons, I am more likely to cut on the straight grain where excess raveling is not much of a problem. All told, either way is good, just be aware of the specific differences of each and adjust to suit yourself and the project.

BIRD HEADS

When appliquéing the head area, the edges that meet the beak need to be turned under whether you appliqué the beak or embroider it. The embroidery should not be considered an appliqué piece that would cover the raw edge of another.

BEAKS

Large beaks can be appliquéd in two pieces, although others are too small (if appliquéd, the work is tedious and a fine point is difficult to achieve). For these embroidery is best.

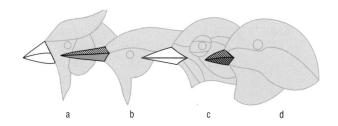

Appliqué the larger beaks, such as on the grosbeaks, in two pieces (a). Or for a medium beak, such as on the redwings, appliqué one piece first. Then satin stitch over the top half to give definition (b), or stem stitch a line that separates as a center (c). Satin stitch the little song bird beaks in two colors (d). Use the lighter color for the top of the beak as the light shows there first. Begin the embroidery at the head and work out to the point.

EYES

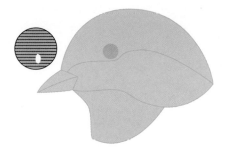

Use a satin stitch to embroider a circle. If the bird's eye has a ring around it, such as the killdeer, add this with a stem stitch. And remember to dot the eyes. A single stitch in the center, or slightly off-center of the eye adds a life-like quality. Use white or other light color for good contrast.

BRANCHES

Cut branches with a general bias or slightly off-grain direction. The greater the curve, the closer to true bias to cut the branch. When appliquéing branches do not make the edges perfectly straight or perfectly even in width. Branches have lumps and bumps.

FEET AND LEGS

For the legs I use a satin stitch and for the toes a stem stitch. Use one or two rows for the feet, curling the toes around the branch the bird is sitting upon. If you don't like stitching toes, just place a leaf, stone, or branch across them. No problems now.

BERRIES

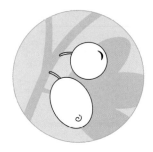

Berries need a little dot (French knot) or a small crescent in stem stitch in a contrasting color or a light hue of the same color of the berry. This little accent adds a lot of interest and dimension.

CHAPTER THREE

Quilting and Finishing

M*y quilting is generally random and asymmetrical in design. I quilt the background and through any borders, leaving the appliqué unquilted. Just before the quilting joins the appliqué, stitch underneath the appliqué piece, between the layers, and come up on the other side. If the appliqué piece covers too large an area to go underneath, end your quilting thread and begin again on the other side.*

BORDERS

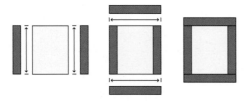

Borders frame the appliquéd picture. You may add one or more borders of varying widths and colors to tie in with your home décor, or select a color from the appliqué. Always measure your appliqué piece and trim to the desired size before adding borders (being sure the borders opposite each other are the same size). I stitch the side borders first and then add the top and bottom borders, stitching straight across. Repeat the order if you add a second border. Use a ¼-inch seam when sewing on the borders.

MARKING

When you first start quilting you tend to mark more designs than you will after you have some experience. The less marking you do, the less you have to remove. I use a water-soluble marker when necessary and always mark very lightly. Designs that will be repeated symmetrically need to be premarked. Using a lightbox, trace your design onto the top of the fabric. Pre-marking is not necessary for random designs. Use a marker lightly or, even better, use the tip of your needle. Draw the needle across the fabric, pressing the tip into the fabric to create a line that will stay long enough for you to quilt the marked line. Just mark as you go. For straight lines use masking tape. I press the tape onto a scrap of fabric first to de-sticky it and then use the tape to mark lines as I stitch. If you need, you can cut small shapes out of masking tape or a non-raveling fabric such as interfacing. Simply pin the shapes to the basted top and quilt around them. For random designs I stitch as if I were doodling, making up the design as I quilt. One area of quilting leads to another: connecting lines or crossing over others can lead to lots of wonderful and unexpected designs. The more you quilt, the less marking you will need.

BASTING THE LAYERS

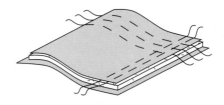

Take the time to do this step well. It will make your quilting smoother and give you a flat quilt once you finish. Cut your backing and batting an inch or so larger than the top. On a smooth surface that you can baste on, lay out the backing, then the batting, and finally the top. Keep the layers smooth and flat. Using white thread, baste a grid of horizontal and vertical lines four inches apart using one-inch-long stitches.

THE QUILTING STITCH

I use a simple running stitch for quilting. As I quilt, I just stitch in and out, taking several stitches on the needle each time (based on the amount of curve in the pattern). I lap quilt without a frame, as this is most comfortable for me.

To begin, knot a 12-inch length of thread—a length much longer will wear the thread as you stitch. Pull the knot through the top into the batting and come up to the top again to begin. To end a thread, put a knot in the thread close to the quilt top and pull it into the batting. Let the needle travel between the layers for an inch or so, then come up and snip. This will leave a tail inside the quilt.

Quilt all the way to the quilt's edge. I continue quilting even through the borders. When you are finished quilting your piece, trim the quilt right to the top's edge, keeping it square. When you add the binding, the quilting will keep all the layers together and help you avoid tucks in the top. Note that close quilting will make the finished quilt a bit smaller than the unfinished top.

QUILTING DESIGNS

Now your piece is ready to quilt. Where to begin quilting and what to quilt are the questions. Quilting stitches illustrate movement of the wind, the shining rays of the sun, or the zipping paths of insects above the fields. There is no end to the combinations of patterns. The stitches can even radiate the vibrancy and life from the birds themselves. Best of all, quilting adds depth and texture with the highlights and shadows created by the quilting lines. Many of my designs begin by highlighting the star of the quilt and that would be the bird or birds. Try radiating lines from the bird, keeping them random lengths and alternating long

and short. Many different shapes and lines could be used to suggest sound. Echo lines are a great choice. These lines follow the shape of the appliqué or quilting and keep going outward with 1/4 inch or so spacing.

Begin feathers with a main vane, either curved or straight. Then starting at the top draw vanes, growing larger or staying the same size as you go down the feather. I do not plan each feather but let it grow as I sew. With a bit of practice they are fun and easy and make wonderfully rich designs. It does help somewhat to start quilting in the center of your quilt if the design permits, but if your basting was done well you can begin anywhere and quilt from any direction.

You may wish to create your own design library for easy idea reference. Or, grab some paper and doodle away. Save the designs you like and put them on index cards for reference. I have included some doodles, which you can use to start a design (pages 16-17). But, keep your eyes on everything and you will soon find designs everywhere.

BINDING

Binding is the finished edge on your quilt. Most of my quilts are square or rectangular and I use single-fold straight-grain binding. If you create a quilt with curved edges, use a bias-cut binding. All the projects require no more than 1/4 yard for binding. I cut the strips two-inches wide, selvage to selvage, using a rotary cutter, ruler, and mat. Folowing the same order as the borders, I stitch the binding on the sides, then the top and bottom. I use a 1/2 inch seam allowance, which makes a finished binding width of 1/2 inch. Turn the binding to the back and, turning under the raw edge 1/2 inch, blind stitch it down, being careful not to let any stitches go through to the front. I pin the entire binding in place before stitching it down on the back.

Always sign and date your finished piece.

CHAPTER FOUR

Twenty-Five Birds
to Appliqué

T*he following bird patterns are numbered for appliqué and include any necessary special instructions. I chose birds for their variety, selecting a range in color and varying body shapes, to include those species that we hold near-and-dear to our hearts. May your favorite feathered friend be among them.*

DESIGNING YOUR OWN PATTERNS

Adapting these birds into worlds of your own design is fun and easy. You will need a few supplies: a lightbox or tracing paper, sharp scissors, an eraser, and a fine-line black marker. For color you can use crayons, colored pencils, or a simple box of children's watercolors. Begin with the basic bird patterns (often I use half size drawing for design) and add flora. You may easily move the birds about, drop a handful of pebbles on the ground, or fill a tree with ripened berries. After I finish a design I either re-draw it at full-size or enlarge it at a print shop.

To begin, first decide the size of the project. Smaller projects are best for those of you just learning to appliqué. After you have some experience, you can move on to larger and more complex designs. From little wallhangings to pillows to a bird on a vest, small projects abound. I find myself with many more designs created than time to appliqué them. What fun!

Your design can revolve around one bird (bring his natural habitat and food into the picture, or add a forest of branches with various birds among the leaves). I recommend a few reference books on birds for inspiration and information on their habits and habitats. Or put out a feeder and use your own observations for project ideas. Better yet, grab a pair of binoculars and go bird watching. Not only will you be filled with possible designs but also find it is a whole lot of fun.

"look straight"

old line

"look down"

"look forward"

I have included some leaf patterns in the projects, but you can easily find basic books on trees and plants for more information. The best leaf pattern is the real leaf. Place it between two pieces of white paper and trace the outline using a lightbox. The same can be said of branch arrangement. After a windstorm there are lots of fallen branches you can use to help you draw realistically-shaped branches. Of course artist's license allows you to move nature about as you choose. I enjoy adding bright berries to liven up a bird motif, or a flower for color. There is no end to the possibilities.

Birds are active creatures that move about and you can easily move your bird's head, tip him forward, sit him down and so forth. Using tracing paper, cut off the head, tilt or turn and re-attach.

The legs can be repositioned to hold the birds on branches of all angles. The tail can be tilted at different angles and, of course, there is the simple reverse of the bird pattern to give you a different look.

When designing with branches, it is the branches that come first; then a bird alights and finally the leaves and berries grow. You can place everything behind the bird or place some leaves and grasses in front of the bird. I often put leaves in front of the feet and solve the problem of embroidering those toes.

At all times it is easiest to trace the patterns as you add items to your picture. An eraser is helpful when you move pieces in front of others and later need to remove the lines that may initially have been hidden. You can make a wonderful picture even if nothing overlaps. You are in charge!

After I create a design I set it aside for a few days and then glance at it for several more. If I still like it, the coloring is added. If you have done your design in half size this will go quite quickly. The color makes easy reference for fabric selection when appliquéing. A black marker to outline the design will make the tracing onto fabric easier.

Once you start designing you will soon have a pile of great ideas. From little to large, you can put these birds on everything—from clothing to home décor to quilts. Give designing a try and then let the needle fly.

"look back"

REDWING *Blackbird*

F*rom the top of the tallest cattail he proclaims his Spring with a loud "I am here." The marshes fill with the sound of their day-long songs. Bold red and yellow epaulets mark these striking birds, leaving no doubt who has arrived.*

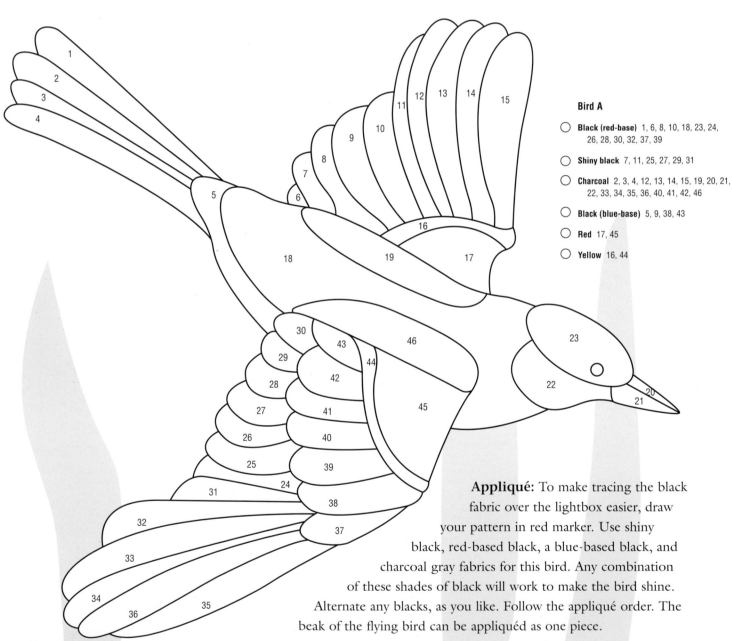

Bird A

○ **Black (red-base)** 1, 6, 8, 10, 18, 23, 24, 26, 28, 30, 32, 37, 39

○ **Shiny black** 7, 11, 25, 27, 29, 31

○ **Charcoal** 2, 3, 4, 12, 13, 14, 15, 19, 20, 21, 22, 33, 34, 35, 36, 40, 41, 42, 46

○ **Black (blue-base)** 5, 9, 38, 43

○ **Red** 17, 45

○ **Yellow** 16, 44

Appliqué: To make tracing the black fabric over the lightbox easier, draw your pattern in red marker. Use shiny black, red-based black, a blue-based black, and charcoal gray fabrics for this bird. Any combination of these shades of black will work to make the bird shine. Alternate any blacks, as you like. Follow the appliqué order. The beak of the flying bird can be appliquéd as one piece.

Embroidery: Satin stitch the eye in medium gray. Add a white dot to the eye. Satin stitch the legs in black; then stem stitch the toes, curling them around the cattail. For the flying bird, run a line with a stem stitch in black or gray across the beak the same length of the single piece.

Redwings in the Cattails, page 60

Bird B

○ **Black (red-base)** 9, 17, 18, 21, 24, 30, 31, 33, 35, 36, 41

○ **Shiny black** 1, 4, 16, 20, 25, 27, 32, 34, 37, 38

○ **Charcoal** 8, 10, 11, 12, 13, 14, 15, 19, 22, 23, 26, 39, 42

○ **Black (blue-base)** 2, 3, 5, 6, 7, 40

○ **Red** 29, 44

○ **Orange** 45

○ **Yellow** 28, 43

Enlarge birds 5%

EASTERN *Bluebird*

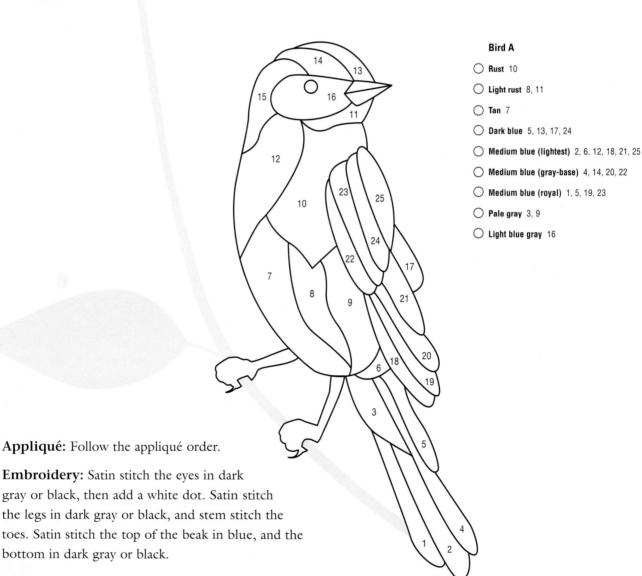

W*e look for his bright blue plumage in the spring. Spotting one on a fence post, we know that winter is now behind us. Bluebirds inhabit open fields and small wooded areas, although many bluebird houses need to be set out to create more nesting sites.*

Bluebird Spring, page 64

Bird A

○ **Rust** 10

○ **Light rust** 8, 11

○ **Tan** 7

○ **Dark blue** 5, 13, 17, 24

○ **Medium blue (lightest)** 2, 6, 12, 18, 21, 25

○ **Medium blue (gray-base)** 4, 14, 20, 22

○ **Medium blue (royal)** 1, 5, 19, 23

○ **Pale gray** 3, 9

○ **Light blue gray** 16

Appliqué: Follow the appliqué order.

Embroidery: Satin stitch the eyes in dark gray or black, then add a white dot. Satin stitch the legs in dark gray or black, and stem stitch the toes. Satin stitch the top of the beak in blue, and the bottom in dark gray or black.

Bird B

○ **Rust** 5

○ **Light rust** —

○ **Tan** 4

○ **Dark blue** 6, 10, 19, 27

○ **Medium blue (lightest** 7, 15, 17, 20, 23, 25

○ **Medium blue (gray-base)** 9, 11, 14, 22

○ **Medium blue (royal)** 8, 12, 13, 18, 21, 24

○ **Pale gray** 1, 2, 3

○ **Light blue gray** 16, 26

Framed Trio, page 54

EASTERN *Blue Jay*

This beautifully colored bird has a habit of being very noisy throughout the woods. Bold at the feeder, you'll see him taking as many sunflower seeds as he can. Yet, the bright blue is a welcome spot of color on winter days, and he is welcome to the seeds.

Appliqué: Appliqué a stem for the jay to sit upon. Follow the appliqué order. The beak is appliquéd in one piece. Cut the entire wing and tail pieces that have the stripes across, and appliqué. Embroider the black stripes.

Embroidery: Use a stem stitch in black for the line through the eye. Satin stitch the eye and legs in black; stem stitch the toes. Use two lines of stem stitch in black for wing and tail stripes. Using a satin stitch, over-embroider the top of the beak in a gray lighter or darker than the appliqué fabric.

Enlarge
bird 10%

○ **White** 4, 7, 10, 12, 14, 16, 18, 20, 27, 28, 36, 39, 45

○ **Black** 33, 44

○ **Pale Gray** 2, 42

○ **Gray** 1, 3, 41

○ **Light blue** 8, 13, 19, 22, 24, 32, 43, 47

○ **Royal blue** 6, 26, 29, 31, 34, 37, 40, 46

○ **Dark blue** 5, 9, 11, 17, 25, 30, 35, 38

○ **Light bluish gray** 15, 21, 23

PAINTED *Bunting*

Little Totes, page 50

T*he gaudy little bunting spends most of his time in thick brush. Perhaps he knows his painted beauty would draw too much attention. A brightly colored bird, he is perfect for appliqué with his decorative coat.*

Appliqué: Follow appliqué order.

Embroidery: Satin stitch the eye in black. Then surround with two rounds of stem stitch in red. Add a white dot. Satin stitch the legs in black, then stem stitch the toes. Satin stitch the top of the beak in light gray, and the bottom in dark gray or black.

- ○ **Brown** 4, 6, 10, 13
- ○ **Bright blue** 23
- ○ **Medium blue** 25
- ○ **Bright-light green** 9, 20, 22, 24
- ○ **Leaf green** 19, 21
- ○ **Medium dark green** 12, 17
- ○ **Olive green** 7, 11, 14, 15, 16, 18
- ○ **Rust** 5
- ○ **Turkey red** 1, 2, 8
- ○ **Bright red** 3

NORTHERN *Cardinal*

Framed Trio, page 54

H*e is bright red, no doubt, with a spirited strong song – the favorite bird of many a bird-watcher. We always know the tomato worms are in the garden when the cardinals gather on the fence. They also dine happily at feeders featuring sunflower seeds.*

Appliqué: Follow the appliqué order.

Embroidery: Satin stitch the legs in black; stem stitch the toes. Satin stitch the eye in black and stem stitch a circle of red using a single strand of floss. Add a white dot to the eye.

○ **Brightest red** 4, 28
○ **Bright red** 16, 17, 18, 22, 24, 27
○ **Turkey red** 3, 5, 9, 15, 19, 21, 26
○ **Rusty red** 6, 8, 10, 12, 13, 20, 23
○ **Rust** 1, 7, 11, 14
○ **Pale rust** 2
○ **Black** 25

BLACK-CAPPED *Chickadee*

Five in the Forest, page 70

Where there is one, there are several. They rush to the feeder to retrieve one seed and zip to a branch to break it open and eat. Then dart back again. Even in the fiercest winter storm they come to the feeder.

Appliqué: Follow the appliqué order. Note that on Bird B, the branch is appliquéd over the finished bird.

Embroidery: Satin stitch the eyes in gray, then add a dot of white. Satin stitch the legs in brown, stem stitch the toes. Note on Bird B that the feet are reaching around the branch from the front, but you can position them as you like with these agile birds. Satin stitch the top of the beaks in brown and the bottom in gray.

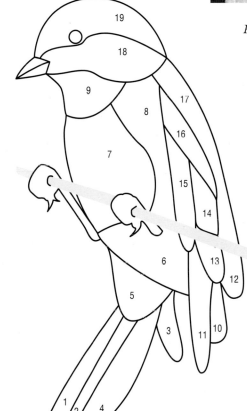

Bird B
- Black 9, 19
- White 7, 13, 16, 18
- Tan 2, 5, 6, 8
- Gray 12, 15, 17
- Brown 3, 10, 14
- Light beige 1
- Very light brown 4, 11

Bird A
- Black 9, 10
- White 5, 8, 14, 18
- Tan 2, 6
- Gray 4, 7, 11, 13, 16
- Brown 3, 12, 17, 19
- Light beige —
- Very light brown 15

SANDHILL *Crane*

I see them in the spring and summer feeding in the fields. Sometimes I view a pair with one young, other times in groups of juvenile birds of five or more. A stately bird, standing four feet or more in height, it has a long shrill cry that rings through the air. Once you hear one you will always recognize this wild sound.

As requested, I've included the Sandhill Crane from Wildflowers, page 79

Appliqué: Follow the appliqué order.

Embroidery: Add a white dot to the eye if you wish.

See pattern pullout for full-size crane

See perforated pattern page for full–size pattern.

AMERICAN *Goldfinch*

The Cat and the Canaries, page 67

In the spring there is no more glorious a yellow than that of the bright feathers on this little "wild canary." What delight when a flock settles to feed on the seeds of dandelion and thistle. There is no mistaking these little fellows.

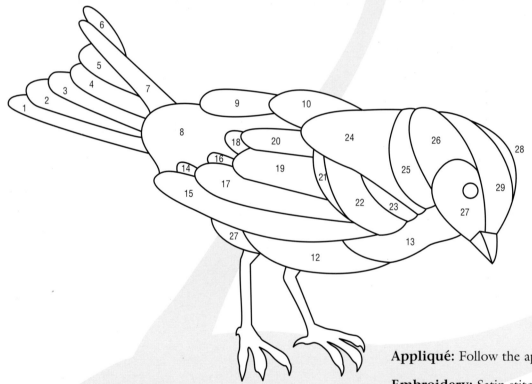

Appliqué: Follow the appliqué order.

Embroidery: Satin stitch the eye in black or dark gray, then add a white dot. Satin stitch the legs in brown or gray, and stem stitch the toes. Satin stitch the top of the beak in peach, and the bottom in beige.

○ **Bright yellow** 13, 24, 26

○ **Yellow** 12, 25, 27

○ **Black** 1, 3, 5, 10, 15, 19, 22, 29

○ **Charcoal** 2, 7, 9, 16, 20, 28

○ **White** 4, 6, 14, 17, 18, 21, 23

○ **Pale gray** 8, 11

EVENING *Grosbeak*

Feathered Stars, page 73

They flock to my feeder in the winter, eating the sunflower seeds in record time. This bird's big and bold beak lends itself to appliqué quite well.

Appliqué: Follow the appliqué order.

Embroidery: Satin stitch the eye in gray, then add a white dot. Satin stitch the legs in gray or beige, and stem stitch the toes.

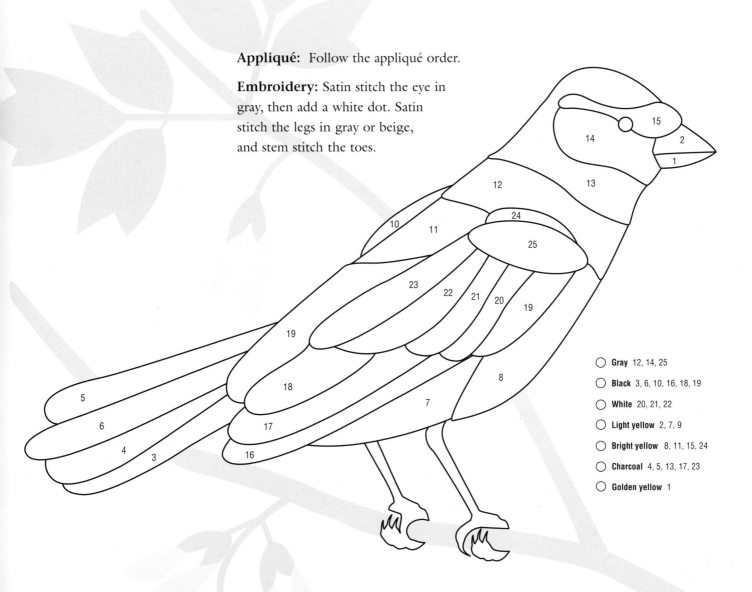

○ **Gray** 12, 14, 25

○ **Black** 3, 6, 10, 16, 18, 19

○ **White** 20, 21, 22

○ **Light yellow** 2, 7, 9

○ **Bright yellow** 8, 11, 15, 24

○ **Charcoal** 4, 5, 13, 17, 23

○ **Golden yellow** 1

ROSE-BREASTED *Grosbeak*

A *large pale beak and a rose-red breast name this creature. In flight its pink wing-linings are visible from below. Often the brightly colored male sits upon the nest and sings! He has a long broken warble.*

Feathered Stars, page 73

○ **White** 2, 3, 6, 7, 9, 16, 17, 18, 19, 20, 21, 38, 54, 55, 56, 57, 58, 59

○ **Medium gray (first)** 13, 14, 15, 26, 42, 43, 44, 45

○ **Medium gray (second)** 10, 11, 12, 46, 47, 48, 52, 53

○ **Beige** 22, 23, 24, 25

○ **Charcoal** 1, 4, 5, 27, 28, 29, 40, 41, 49, 50, 51, 61, 62, 63

○ **Rose** 33, 39, 60, 68, 69, 70, 71, 72, 73

○ **Black** 8, 30, 31, 32, 34, 37, 64, 65, 66, 67, 74, 75

○ **Tan** 36

○ **Dark tan** 35

Enlarge bird 20%

Appliqué: Follow the appliqué order.

Embroidery: Satin stitch the eye in gray, then add a white dot.

Hummingbirds

We all love these tiny creatures. Their antics amuse us; red flowers attract them. When they arrive in the spring they come to my window to ask that the feeder be filled. I gladly oblige. Mine are not a specific species, though I used a ruby-throated bird as a model.

Hummingbirds and Fuchsia, page 57

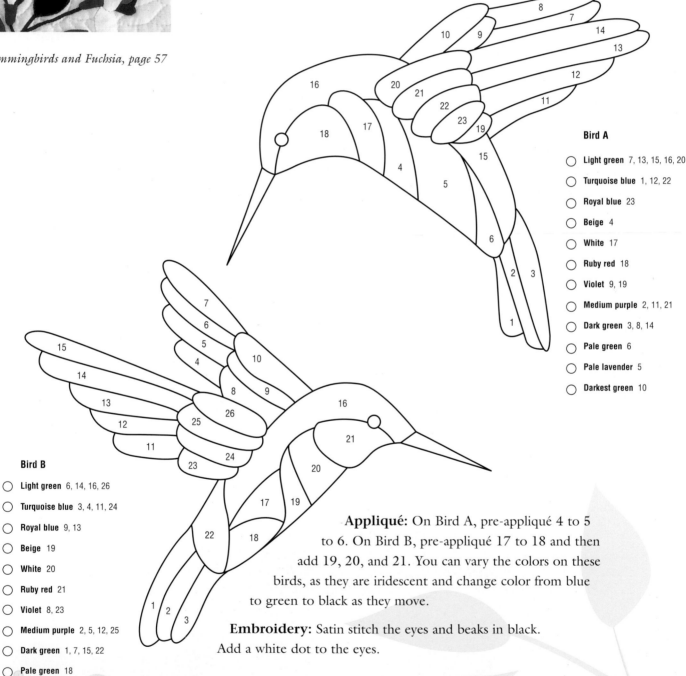

Bird A

○ **Light green** 7, 13, 15, 16, 20

○ **Turquoise blue** 1, 12, 22

○ **Royal blue** 23

○ **Beige** 4

○ **White** 17

○ **Ruby red** 18

○ **Violet** 9, 19

○ **Medium purple** 2, 11, 21

○ **Dark green** 3, 8, 14

○ **Pale green** 6

○ **Pale lavender** 5

○ **Darkest green** 10

Bird B

○ **Light green** 6, 14, 16, 26

○ **Turquoise blue** 3, 4, 11, 24

○ **Royal blue** 9, 13

○ **Beige** 19

○ **White** 20

○ **Ruby red** 21

○ **Violet** 8, 23

○ **Medium purple** 2, 5, 12, 25

○ **Dark green** 1, 7, 15, 22

○ **Pale green** 18

○ **Darkest green** 10

○ **Pale lavender** 17

Appliqué: On Bird A, pre-appliqué 4 to 5 to 6. On Bird B, pre-appliqué 17 to 18 and then add 19, 20, and 21. You can vary the colors on these birds, as they are iridescent and change color from blue to green to black as they move.

Embroidery: Satin stitch the eyes and beaks in black. Add a white dot to the eyes.

NORTHERN *Junco*

O*r, the Oregon Junco…also called the Snowbird. These birds appear at the feeder as the weather begins to cool and snowflakes fall. Ground feeders, these birds are fond of weed seeds and cracked corn at a low feeder.*

Pastel Leaves on Point, page 52

○ **Black** 20, 22
○ **White** 1, 4, 8
○ **Tan** 2
○ **Dark tan** 3
○ **Charcoal** 11, 21
○ **Medium brown (first)** 6, 10, 13, 15, 17
○ **Medium brown (second)** 5, 7, 9, 12, 14, 19
○ **Dark brown** 16, 18

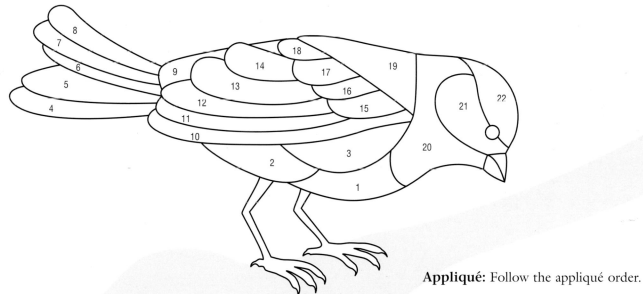

Appliqué: Follow the appliqué order.

Embroidery: Satin stitch the eye in gray, then add a white dot. Satin stitch the legs in beige or brown, and stem stitch the toes. Satin stitch the top of the beak in gray and the bottom in beige.

Killdeer

These noisy birds call their own name. They do not build nests, preferring instead to lay their eggs in the shallow depressions among stone or grassy areas. The killdeer's diet is comprised mainly of insects from the field. A red eye-ring is visible at close view.

Two Killdeer, page 62

Appliqué: Follow the appliqué order.

Embroidery: Satin stitch the eye in black, surrounding the black with a line of red stem stitch. Add a white dot to the eye. Satin stitch the legs in white at the top, and in beige at the bottom. Stem stitch the toes. Satin stitch the top of the beak in dark gray or brown and the bottom in black.

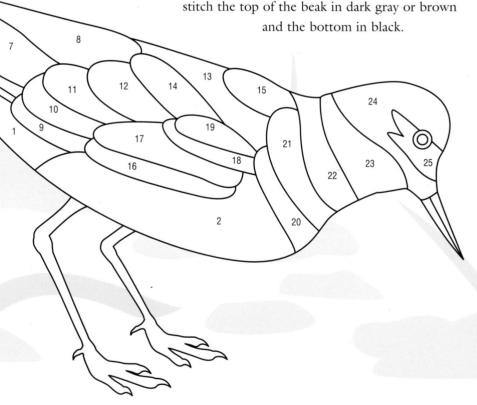

Enlarge birds 10%

○ **White** 2, 21, 23, 25

○ **Tan** 8, 9, 10, 11, 14, 15, 16, 17, 18, 19, 24

○ **Black** 6, 20, 22

○ **Yellow gold** 5

○ **Pale beige** 1, 3

○ **Rusty tan** 12, 14

○ **Pale brownish gray** 7

○ **Dark brown** 4

Meadowlark

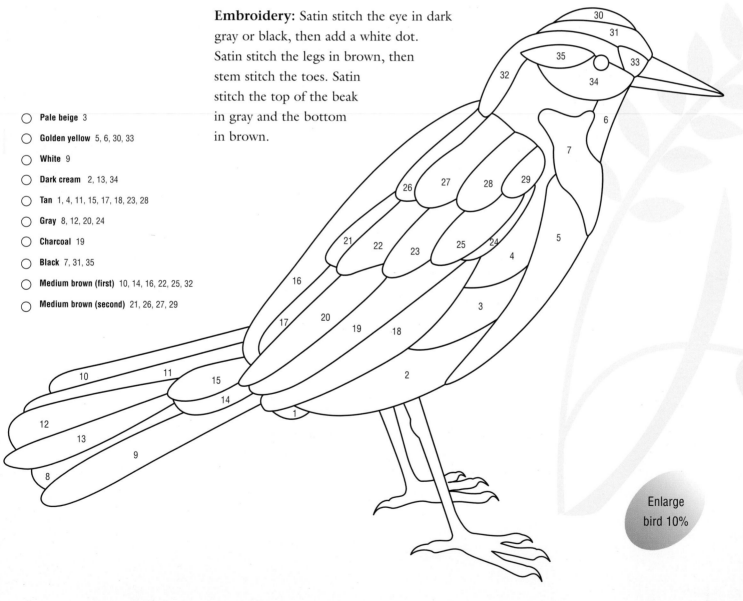

The Eastern and Western meadowlarks are nearly identical save for their song. Living in open fields, pastures, and prairies, a meadowlark is frequently sighted atop a post or wire.

Feathered Stars, page 73

Appliqué: Follow the appliqué order.

Embroidery: Satin stitch the eye in dark gray or black, then add a white dot. Satin stitch the legs in brown, then stem stitch the toes. Satin stitch the top of the beak in gray and the bottom in brown.

○ **Pale beige** 3
○ **Golden yellow** 5, 6, 30, 33
○ **White** 9
○ **Dark cream** 2, 13, 34
○ **Tan** 1, 4, 11, 15, 17, 18, 23, 28
○ **Gray** 8, 12, 20, 24
○ **Charcoal** 19
○ **Black** 7, 31, 35
○ **Medium brown (first)** 10, 14, 16, 22, 25, 32
○ **Medium brown (second)** 21, 26, 27, 29

Enlarge bird 10%

WHITE-THROATED *Nuthatch*

Quite an acrobat, although the largest of its family, this bird is constantly on the go. He hangs upside-down on the feeder. On trees he searches, head down, along the bark for insects. Fond of suet he is a constant visitor to my feeding station in the winter.

Five in the Forest, page 70

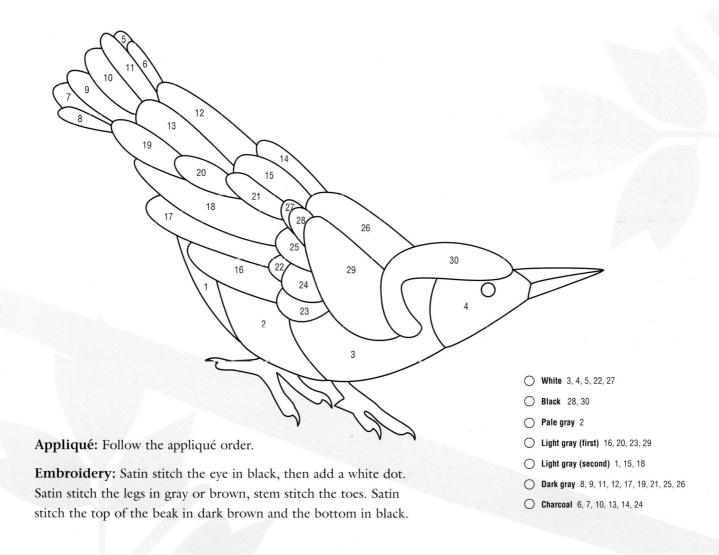

Appliqué: Follow the appliqué order.

Embroidery: Satin stitch the eye in black, then add a white dot. Satin stitch the legs in gray or brown, stem stitch the toes. Satin stitch the top of the beak in dark brown and the bottom in black.

○ **White** 3, 4, 5, 22, 27

○ **Black** 28, 30

○ **Pale gray** 2

○ **Light gray (first)** 16, 20, 23, 29

○ **Light gray (second)** 1, 15, 18

○ **Dark gray** 8, 9, 11, 12, 17, 19, 21, 25, 26

○ **Charcoal** 6, 7, 10, 13, 14, 24

BALTIMORE *Oriole*

Now known as the Northern Oriole, this bird was named for Lord Baltimore (its color matches the Lord's family crest). Chopped fruit or an orange half may bring them to your feeder. Often, they visit hummingbird feeders.

Feathered Stars, page 73

Appliqué: Add a stem first for the bird to sit upon. Then follow the appliqué order for the bird.

Embroidery: Satin stitch the eye in gray, then add a white dot. Satin stitch the legs in black, and stem stitch the toes. Satin stitch the top of the beak in gray or brown, the bottom in black.

○ **Black**   1, 14, 16, 18, 20, 24, 25, 27
○ **White**   15, 22
○ **Charcoal**   13, 17, 19, 21, 26, 28
○ **Golden orange**   4, 5, 23
○ **Bright orange**   3, 7, 11
○ **Orange**   2, 6, 8, 9, 10, 12

Robin

This is the best known bird in the country. We always vie to be the first to sight this harbinger of spring. Its rusty cinnamon-brown breast easily identifies this familiar friend on our lawns. Its beautiful warbling song tells us of the warming earth and fades the chill of the long North Country winter.

Framed Trio, page 54

- ○ **Rusty red** 1
- ○ **Medium Rust** 3
- ○ **Light Rust** 4
- ○ **Golden yellow** 7
- ○ **White** 6, 11* (eye)
- ○ **Light gray** 18, 19, 20, 25, 35
- ○ **Dark gray** 5, 8, 13, 15, 17, 23, 26, 27, 28, 33
- ○ **Charcoal** 10, 12, 14, 21, 22, 24, 29, 30, 31, 34
- ○ **Blue gray** 9, 16, 32, 11* (eye)
- ○ **Light brownish gray** 2

*11 eye detail

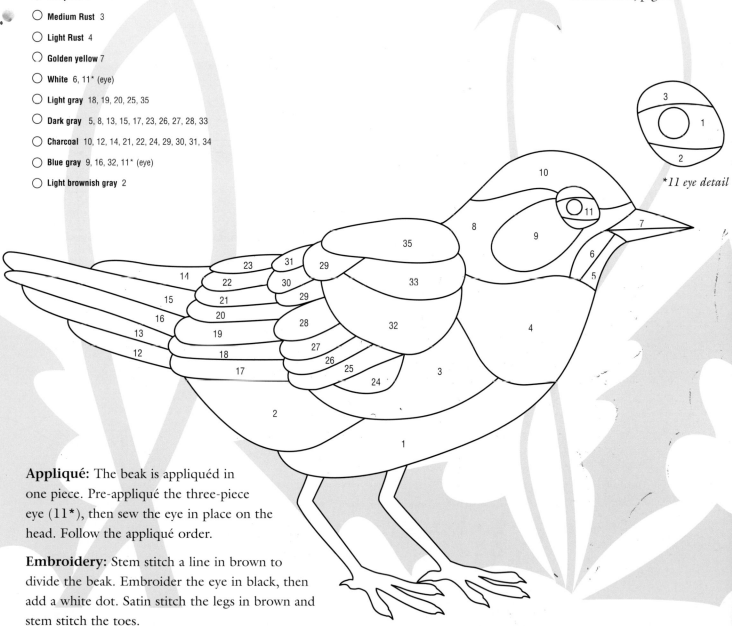

Appliqué: The beak is appliquéd in one piece. Pre-appliqué the three-piece eye (11*), then sew the eye in place on the head. Follow the appliqué order.

Embroidery: Stem stitch a line in brown to divide the beak. Embroider the eye in black, then add a white dot. Satin stitch the legs in brown and stem stitch the toes.

WHITE-THROATED *Sparrow*

D*istinctive yellow eye patches and a white throat mark these melodious singers. They spend much of their time on the ground searching noisily for their food; echoes within the dry leaves make them sound much larger than their size.*

Little Totes, page 50

○ **Black** 11
○ **White** 7, 9, 10. 13, 23, 24, 25
○ **Pale gray** 8
○ **Gray** 15
○ **Yellow** 14
○ **Tan** 6
○ **Dark tan** 5
○ **Pinkish tan** 20, 28
○ **Medium brown (first)** 1, 4, 12, 16, 18, 21, 26, 29
○ **Medium brown (second)** 2, 3, 17, 22
○ **Rust brown** 19, 27

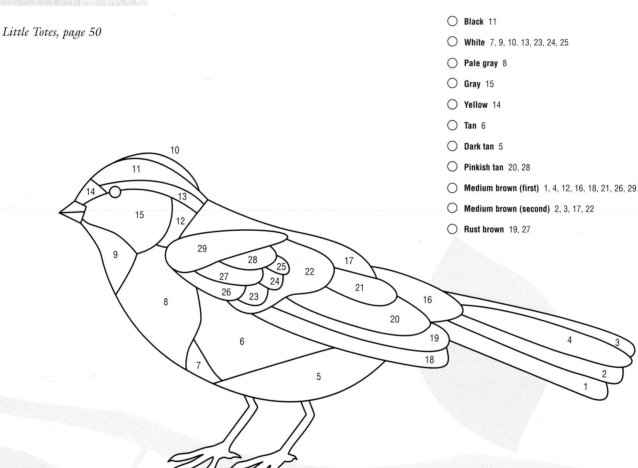

Appliqué: Follow the appliqué order.

Embroidery: Satin stitch the eye in gray, then add a white dot. Satin stitch the legs in gray or beige, and stem stitch the toes.

CLIFF *Swallow*

These insect-eating birds build mud nests on rocky cliffs, though they move quite readily to the eaves of barns, sheds, and even houses. We applaud their love of gnats and mosquitoes in our North Country. They dart and sail about as they catch their dinner mid-air.

Five in the Forest, page 70

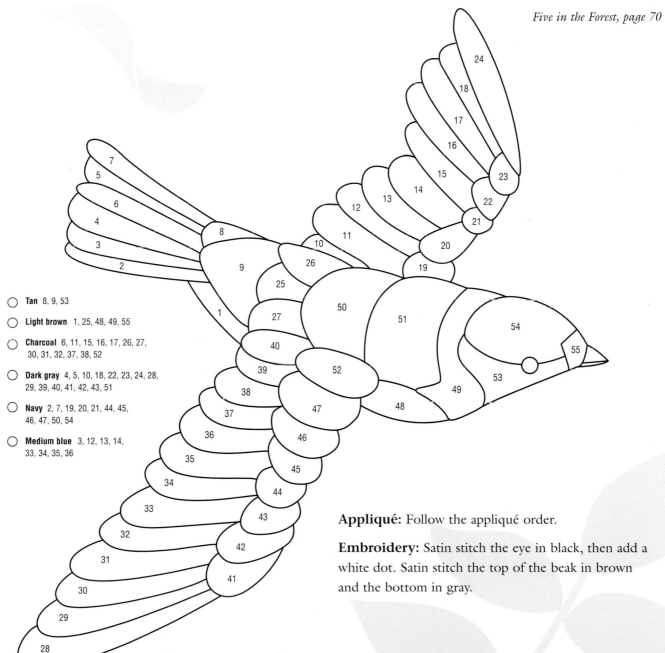

○ **Tan** 8, 9, 53

○ **Light brown** 1, 25, 48, 49, 55

○ **Charcoal** 6, 11, 15, 16, 17, 26, 27, 30, 31, 32, 37, 38, 52

○ **Dark gray** 4, 5, 10, 18, 22, 23, 24, 28, 29, 39, 40, 41, 42, 43, 51

○ **Navy** 2, 7, 19, 20, 21, 44, 45, 46, 47, 50, 54

○ **Medium blue** 3, 12, 13, 14, 33, 34, 35, 36

Appliqué: Follow the appliqué order.

Embroidery: Satin stitch the eye in black, then add a white dot. Satin stitch the top of the beak in brown and the bottom in gray.

SCARLET *Tanager*

Imagine the joy at sighting his bright plumage on a summer day. An Eastern bird, occasional to the West, he loves a diet of insects but does enjoy fruits and berries.

Feathered Stars, page 73

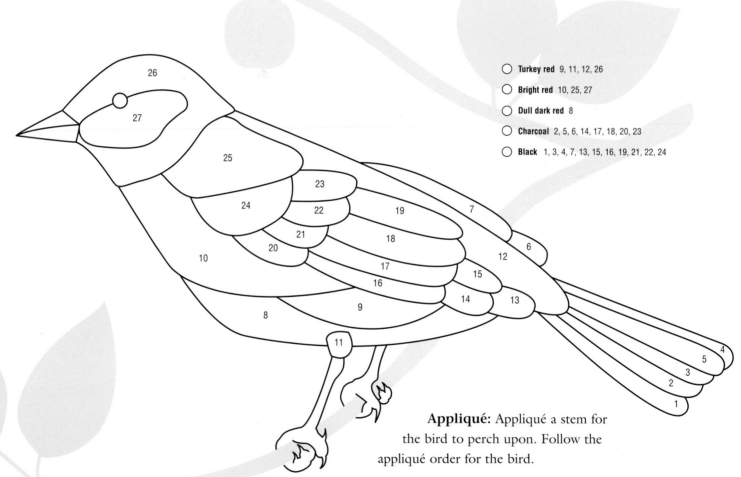

○ **Turkey red** 9, 11, 12, 26
○ **Bright red** 10, 25, 27
○ **Dull dark red** 8
○ **Charcoal** 2, 5, 6, 14, 17, 18, 20, 23
○ **Black** 1, 3, 4, 7, 13, 15, 16, 19, 21, 22, 24

Appliqué: Appliqué a stem for the bird to perch upon. Follow the appliqué order for the bird.

Embroidery: Satin stitch both legs and the eye in black. Add a white dot to the eye. Satin stitch the top of the beak in medium brown and the bottom in black. Stem stitch the toes.

TUFTED *Titmouse*

A*s a child these were my favorite little birds at the feeder. They flit to-and-fro, even hanging upside down. Bold little fellows, they will take food from your hand if you are patient.*

Pastel Leaves on Point, page 52

Appliqué: Follow the appliqué order.

Embroidery: Satin stitch the legs in beige; stem stitch the toes. Satin stitch the eye in black, then add a dot of white. Sew the top of the beak in black and the bottom in gray, using a satin stitch.

○ **Blue gray** 18
○ **Light gray** 13
○ **Pale gray** 15
○ **Dark gray** 7, 19
○ **Greenish gray** 11, 17
○ **Gray** 6, 9
○ **Gray (first)** 6, 9
○ **White** 1, 14
○ **Charcoal** 4, 8, 16
○ **Gray (second)** 5, 10, 12, 20
○ **Pale cream** 2
○ **Pale tan** 3

BLACK-THROATED BLUE *Warbler*

T*his woodland warbler lives among a thick undergrowth of woods, where it vies for insect life. There are many warblers, most of which bear yellow markings. This warbler exhibits a change from the more common coloring.*

Pastel Leaves on Point, page 52

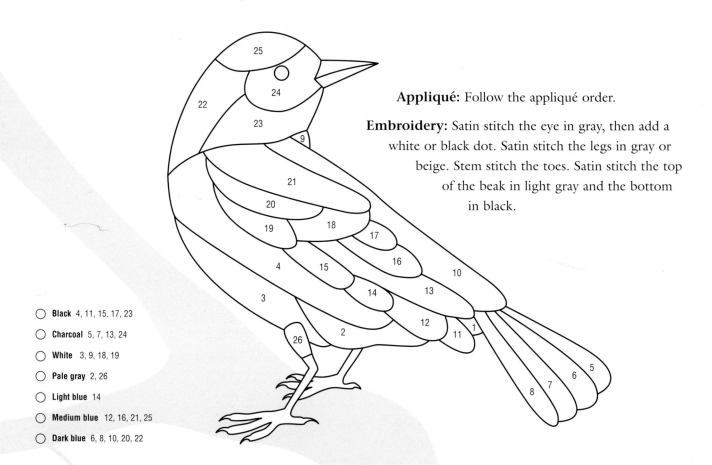

Appliqué: Follow the appliqué order.

Embroidery: Satin stitch the eye in gray, then add a white or black dot. Satin stitch the legs in gray or beige. Stem stitch the toes. Satin stitch the top of the beak in light gray and the bottom in black.

○ **Black** 4, 11, 15, 17, 23

○ **Charcoal** 5, 7, 13, 24

○ **White** 3, 9, 18, 19

○ **Pale gray** 2, 26

○ **Light blue** 14

○ **Medium blue** 12, 16, 21, 25

○ **Dark blue** 6, 8, 10, 20, 22

CEDAR *Waxwing*

Feathered Stars, page 73

Waxwings search for fruit and berries, travelling in flocks except in nesting season. Red waxy wingtips give this bird its name. We often have groups appear when our wild sugarplums and cherries are ripe.

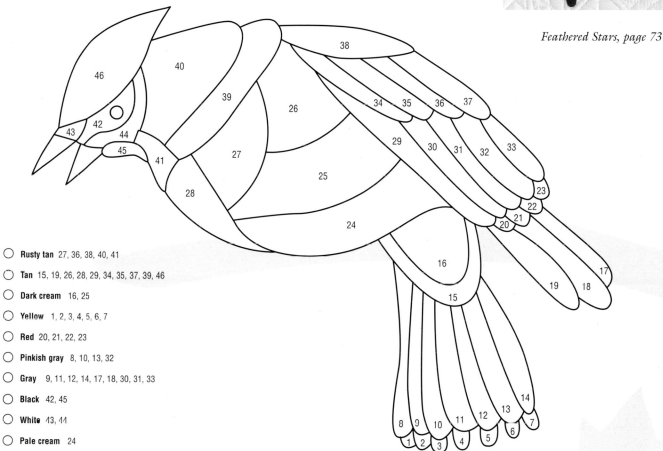

○ **Rusty tan** 27, 36, 38, 40, 41

○ **Tan** 15, 19, 26, 28, 29, 34, 35, 37, 39, 46

○ **Dark cream** 16, 25

○ **Yellow** 1, 2, 3, 4, 5, 6, 7

○ **Red** 20, 21, 22, 23

○ **Pinkish gray** 8, 10, 13, 32

○ **Gray** 9, 11, 12, 14, 17, 18, 30, 31, 33

○ **Black** 42, 45

○ **White** 43, 44

○ **Pale cream** 24

Appliqué: Appliqué a stem first. Follow the appliqué order. Take your time stitching the tiny feathered tips.

Embroidery: Satin stitch the eyes in brown or beige, then add a white dot. Satin stitch the top and bottom beak in black.

RED-HEADED *Woodpecker*

Although an easily identifiable woodpecker this bird is not abundant within its range due to habitat loss and competition from starlings for nest cavities. Their heads are entirely red. They store food in cavities and cracks in trees, but much of this food is never retrieved. Like many other woodpeckers, they will come to a suet feeder.

Five in the Forest, page 70

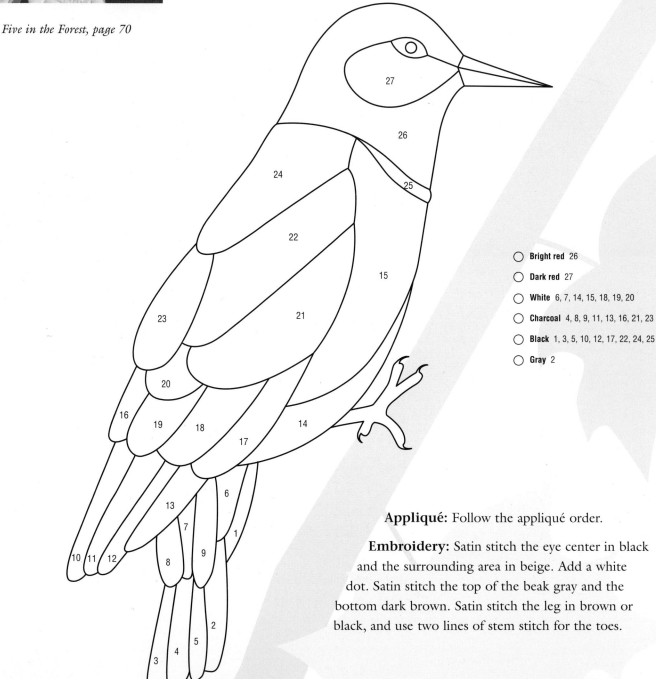

○ **Bright red** 26

○ **Dark red** 27

○ **White** 6, 7, 14, 15, 18, 19, 20

○ **Charcoal** 4, 8, 9, 11, 13, 16, 21, 23

○ **Black** 1, 3, 5, 10, 12, 17, 22, 24, 25

○ **Gray** 2

Appliqué: Follow the appliqué order.

Embroidery: Satin stitch the eye center in black and the surrounding area in beige. Add a white dot. Satin stitch the top of the beak gray and the bottom dark brown. Satin stitch the leg in brown or black, and use two lines of stem stitch for the toes.

CAROLINA *Wren*

This is the largest member of its family. It is a seldom-seen bird that darts about in brushy trees. The white streak over the eye is its most noticeable marking. Heard more than seen, the wren's commonest sound resembles "tea kettle, tea kettle."

Five in the Forest, page 70

○ **White** 10, 12

○ **Medium brown (first)** 2, 5

○ **Medium brown (second)** 11, 15, 18

○ **Light cinnamon** 19

○ **Medium cinnamon** 9, 13, 17

○ **Light brownish gray** 3, 4, 14, 16, 20

○ **Beige** 7, 8

○ **Dark brown** 1

○ **Dark tan** 6

Appliqué: Follow the appliqué order.

Embroidery: Satin stitch the eye in black, then add a dot of white. Satin stitch the legs in brown, then stem stitch the toes. Satin stitch the top of the beak in light brown and the bottom in dark brown.

Little Totes

*S*imple and colorful, these easy totes can carry any bird you choose. I have chosen the bright and bold Painted Bunting and the White-Throated Sparrow for my totes.

White-Throated Sparrow (page 42)

Painted Bunting (page 25)

Materials

- Muslin for lining and tote front
- Color for straps and tote backs
- Selection of colors for Appliqué
- Matching thread
- Quilting thread in natural color
- Floss: see individual bird patterns
- Batting: 9" x 10½" for each tote front

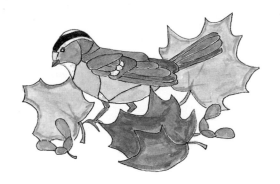

Cutting: per tote

- Muslin tote front and front backing: 10" x 12" Trim to 8½" x 11" after quilting

- Color fabric; for back of tote cut 8½" x 11"

- Muslin tote liner; cut two pieces 8½" x 11"

- Tote handles; cut from any color, two strips 2½" x 14"

Appliqué

Mark your chosen bird 3" or so from the bottom of the background fabric. Appliqué according to the individual bird patterns.

Embroidery

Embroider according to individual bird patterns.
Remove any marker and press from the back. Baste for quilting.

Quilting

Quilt radiating lines in simple designs using masking tape to mark the lines. Remove the basting and trim the piece to 8½" x 11", keeping the bird centered side-to-side and about 2½" from the bottom.

With right sides together (the quilted front and the colored back) stitch around the sides and bottom using a ¼" seam. Turn right side out. Sew the straps together lengthwise to form a tube turn right side out, center seam and press.

Pin the straps to the top edge of the right side of front and back. Sew the side seams of lining with right side together. Slide the lining with the wrong sides still out over the outer bag. Match the side seams. Stitch around the top using a ¼" seam. Pull the lining up and turn under the bottom seam and sew across to close. Push the lining into the bag and quilt or top stitch around the top to keep the lining in place.

Pastel Leaves on Point

Northern Junco, Black-Throated Blue Warbler, and little Tufted Titmouse amid pastel leaves adorn these three on-point squares. The subdued colors soothe, and the small size gives you a beginning at quilting in random designs. A great project to start for those new to appliqué.

Blue Warbler (page 46)
9" x 9" (finished size)

Tufted Titmouse (page 45)
9" x 9" (finished size)

Northern Junco (page 35)
9" x 9" (finished size)

Materials

- Muslin background and backing: two 10" x 10" squares per piece
- Brown fabric for binding: 1/8 yard
- Selection of colors for Appliqué
- Matching thread
- Quilting thread in natural color
- Floss: beige, black, gray, greens
- Batting: 10" x 10"

Cutting

Cut muslin background 10" x 10". Trim to 9½" x 9½" after appliqué and embroidery. Lay out the design to fit the square on-point.

Appliqué

See the individual bird patterns for appliqué order.

Embroidery

Use two rows of stem stitch for the leaf stems. Use single lines of stem stitch for berry stems. Use French knot on each berry in gray. Follow the embroidery directions for each individual bird. Remove any marker. Press and baste for quilting.

Quilting

Northern Junco: Quilt radiating tear drops in two tiers from the bird. Continue outward with large random shells to the edge. Run a line through the middle of each shell, top to bottom.

Tufted Titmouse: Quilt points around the bird and echo the points once. Fill the rest of the quilting area with looping doodling lines.

Blue Warbler: Radiate feather fans outward from the bird. Fill the remaining area with stars made of three intersecting lines. Select habitat from the project of your choice.

Trim to 9" x 9" approximately, making sure the piece is square. Remove the basting. Bind. (See Binding page 15).

Framed Trio

Three of our very recognizable feathered friends are pictured here in simple habitat. Unquilted, the small panels are matted and can be put in wooden frames. Our trio includes: Eastern Bluejay perching in a fruiting maple, Robin standing among the dandelions and Cardinal resting on an autumn aspen branch. You can easily design your own little world for your favorite bird.

Eastern Blue Jay (page 24)
9" x 9" (finished size)

Northern Cardinal (page 26)
9" x 9" (finished size)

Robin (page 41)
9" x 9" (finished size)

Materials

- Muslin for background; 11" x 11" square for each design
- Selection of colors for Appliqué
- Matching thread
- Floss: see individual bird patterns for colors, add greens and cream for habitat
- Batting: 14" x 14" for each design
- Frame and backing board
- Mat: 14" x 14" with a 9" x 9" opening

Appliqué

I designed these motifs to fit in a 9" by 9" opening cut in a mat but you can adjust the designs to fit any size you like.

See the individual bird patterns for their appliqué order. Use bias for grass and dandelion stems. See Bias strips page 11.

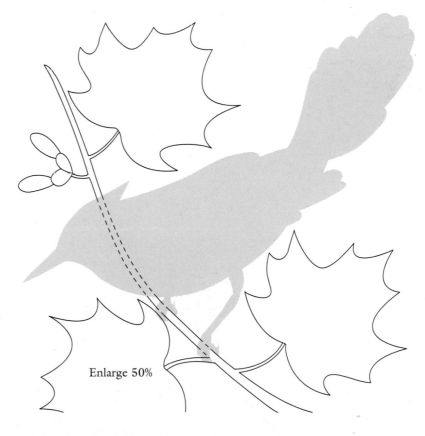

Enlarge 50%

Embroidery

Use a double line of stem stitch in green or brown for leaf stems. Combine a strand of green and a strand of cream together and using a stem stitch, embroider radiating lines to form the dandelion seed head. A few straight stitches at the end of the unopened seed head in the same color combinations will complete the habitat. Follow the embroidery directions for each individual bird.

Remove any marker. Press the appliquéd piece. Use a little spray starch or sizing to keep the piece flat. With a bit of glue, adhere the batting to the frame backing board. Lay the appliqué piece on top and attach with some stitches through the batting or double stick tape. Keep the tape behind the appliqué so that it will not show through the background. Use the same tape to hold the mat in the frame.

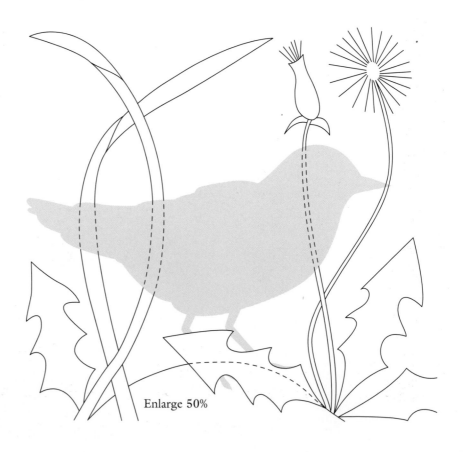

Enlarge 50%

Hummingbirds and Fuchsia

An irresistible project featuring those favorite sprites, the hummingbirds. Looking for supper, these three hover among hanging fuchsia. I find myself wanting to design piece after piece featuring these colorful birds. You will too!

Hummingbirds (page 34) 20" x 28" approx. finished size

Materials

- Muslin background and backing: 1 yard
- Dark green border: ¼ yard
- Navy blue binding: ¼ yard
- Selection of colors for Appliqué
- Matching thread
- Quilting thread in natural color
- Floss: black, green, yellow and white
- Batting: 22" x 30"

Cutting

Cut muslin background 19" x 26". Trim to 17" x 24" after appliqué and embroidery are complete.

Dark green border: cut three strips 2½" wide selvage to selvage. Measure for exact length before you stitch. See Borders page 14.

Navy blue binding: cut three strips 2" wide selvage to selvage. Measure for exact length before you stitch. See Binding page 15.

Lay out the fuchsia vines, growing out from the top and left edges of the top. The stem ends will be caught in the seam when the borders are added. Add leaves of various sizes and flowers and buds, as you like. The highest bird is Bird A and the two lower birds are Bird B, one as is and one reversed.

Appliqué

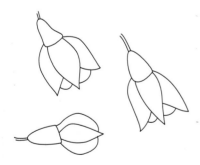

Begin by appliquéing the stems using green bias. See Bias strips page 11. Add the leaves, flowers and buds following the appliqué order shown at left. Use the individual bird patterns for appliqué order for the hummingbirds.

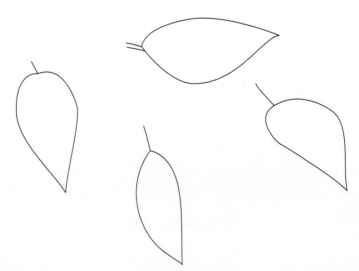

Embroidery

Using a green stem stitch embroider the leaf stems. Stem stitch lines in green, tipped with a yellow French knot for the fuchsia stamens. See individual bird patterns for the hummingbird embroidery.

Remove any markings and press. Trim the piece to 17" x 24" making sure the stem ends are on the edges and will be caught in the 1/4" seam that adds the borders. Add borders. Press and baste for quilting.

Quilting

Begin by quilting echo lines out from the hummingbirds' wings. Add the two large feathers. Radiate lines from each bird on the wing sides filling in the center section. Fill some areas with random shells and others with radiating lines as your mood suits. There is no one right way here. Enjoy yourself. Check the size and trim the quilt to the top's edge keeping it square. Remove the basting and bind. Refer to photograph for reference.

*See large template
on pattern page*

Redwings in the Cattails

S*inging Redwings among the cattails makes a wonderful picture. Working with shades of black offers a bit of a challenge but is rewarding with grand results. The open environment provides a fantastic canvas for quilt design lines. Enjoy the possibilities.*

Redwing Blackbirds (pages 20 and 21) 22½" x 34" (finished size)

Materials

- Muslin background and backing: 2 yards
- Black binding: ¼ yard
- Selection of colors for Appliqué
- Matching thread
- Quilting thread in natural color
- Floss: gray, white, black
- Batting: 25" x 36"

Enlarge
70%

Cutting

Cut muslin background 26" x 37". Trim to 24" x 35" after appliqué and embroidery are complete.

Black binding: cut four strips 2" wide selvage to selvage. Measure for exact length before you stitch. See Binding page 15.

Lay out the cattails along the bottom edge of the design. Add the two blackbirds, one flying and one atop a cattail. Adjust the sitting bird's feet to hold the cattail top.

Appliqué

Appliqué the cattails first. Pre-appliqué the two-piece cattail "flowers" and the two-piece leaves. Sew down the pieces that are behind anything else first, including the stems. Use small bias for the stems. See Bias strips page 11.

See the individual bird patterns for the appliqué order of the blackbirds.

Embroidery

Embroider the birds' details according to the individual bird patterns. Remove any markings and press. Trim to 24" x 35". Baste for quilting.

Quilting

Begin with the circles of song, leaving the sitting bird's mouth and leading toward the flying bird. Break up the sky with large scalloped clouds and echo each cloud line to make four spaces. Fill in the cloud areas with doodling loops in some areas and random triangles in others. Quilt some grass blades upward from the bottom among the cattails. Fill the bottom spaces between the grasses with side-to-side lines. Go upwards two-thirds or so of the grass height. Finish the space downward with random shells, varied with doodling loops. See photograph for reference.

Check the size and trim the quilt to the top's edge, keeping it square. Remove the basting and bind.

Two Killdeer

Two birds with subtle position differences; each searching the pebbles for a snack. The killdeer has stunning crisp color changes in its feathers. I created a bright world despite the basic colors. The dry meadow offers many quilting design options.

Killdeer (pages 36 and 37) 22" x 29 1/2" (finished size)

Materials

- Muslin background and backing: 1 yard
- Tan border: ¼ yard
- Black binding: ¼ yard
- Quilting thread in natural color
- Floss: black, cream, beige, gray, red, green
- Selection of colors for Appliqué
- Batting: 25" x 33"
- Matching thread

Cutting

Cut muslin background 20" x 27". Trim to 17½" x 25" after appliqué and embroidery are complete.

Tan border: cut four strips 2½" wide selvage to selvage. Measure for exact length before you stitch. See Borders page 14.

Black binding: cut four strips 2" wide selvage to selvage. Measure for exact length before you stitch. See Binding page 15.

Lay out your pattern, scattering stones along the bottom, and adding grasses and plantain. Place the birds in front of the plants. Use one of each bird. Bird A on the left and Bird B on the right.

Appliqué

Begin with the stones behind, adding the closer ones as you work forward. Add grasses and plantain, overlapping as you choose. Pre appliqué the two-piece grasses. Use tiny bias for grass stems. See Bias strips page 11. Add the birds last over top of the plants. See individual bird patterns for appliqué order.

Embroidery

See individual bird patterns for embroidery instruction. Use two rows of green stem stitch for the plantain stems. Sew a number of single stitches outward from the plantain flower, adding a French knot in cream at the end of each. Scatter green French knots over the grass heads.

Remove any markings and press. Trim to 17½" x 25" and add border. Press and baste for quilting.

Quilting

Stitch random pebbles across the bottom upward to the appliquéd stones. Quilt a zig-zag star around the birds, stopping at the stones. Echo this line once. Echo the bird's shape within the star shape. Scatter some long bending grass heads. Complete the quilting with random lines in all different directions. See photo for reference. Use masking tape to aid in quilting these straight lines. Avoid running any line parallel with the borders either way. Trim to quilt top's edge, keeping it square. Remove basting and bind.

Enlarge
65%

Bluebird Spring

Spring bursts forth with bright redbuds and flowering dogwoods. Who better to announce the change of season but the Eastern Bluebird? Flowers make a wonderful color addition to the already colorful birds, and flowering trees are perfect for these perching birds. The quilting offers a study in a simple shape, the square, repeated and overlapped.

Bluebirds (pages 22 and 23) 24½" x 33" (finished size)

Materials

- Muslin background and backing: 2 yards
- Medium green binding: ¼ yard
- Selection of colors for Appliqué
- Matching thread

- Floss: green, brown, yellow, dark gray, white, blue
- Quilting thread in natural color
- Batting: 28" x 37"

Cutting

Cut muslin background 27" x 35". Trim to 26" x 34" after appliqué and embroidery are complete.

Medium green binding: cut four strips 2" wide selvage to selvage. Measure for exact length before you stitch. See Binding page 15.

Begin your design with redbud and dogwood branches. Add the birds to sit on the branches. Bird A at the top and Bird B in the bottom right. Add blossoms and leaves.

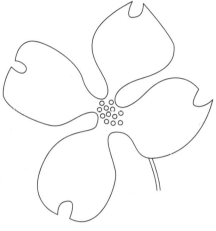

Appliqué

Stitch the small stems first, using bias or off-grain. Follow with the larger branches, noting which goes over the other. Add redbuds and dogwood blossoms. See pattern for appliqué order (on perforated pattern page). Add the leaves, and finally, the birds. See individual bird patterns for appliqué order. The white dogwood blossom can be self-lined (see page 11) to avoid turn-under shadows. Work slowly with the tight inside curves of the dogwoods. See Inside Curves page 11.

Embroidery

Two rows of brown stem stitch for the redbud stems and two rows, one green and one brown for the dogwood flower stems. A single line of green stem stitch for the leaf stems. A cluster of French knots in green, yellow, and brown fill the centers of the dogwood blossoms. With the same colors, use single stitches ending in a French knot for the partially opened dogwood flowers. Refer to the individual bird patterns for bluebird embroidery.

Remove any markings and press. Trim to 26" x 34" keeping it square and baste for quilting.

Quilting

Highlight the birds first. Radiate lines from the rough center of the birds outward. Alternate the length of the lines; long, short, long, short around. Use masking tape to keep these lines straight. Connect all the ends with straight lines and a star is formed. Echo the outside line of this star once. Cluster some veined leaves along the branches in random fashion. The remaining areas are filled with overlapping $1^1/2$" squares. Cut a $1^1/2$" square from masking tape or non-raveling fabric. Quilt all around the square, each time overlapping it across the open areas. Try playing on a piece of paper at first to get the feel of this pattern. See photo for reference.

Trim the quilt up to the top's edge, keeping it square and approx. 25" x $33^1/2$". Remove the basting and bind.

Enlarge
70%

The Cat and Three "Canaries"

I*could not help but have fun with our American Goldfinch. A naughty cat is certainly considering these three wild canaries for lunch. Combined with a lively quilting pattern and a brightly blooming trumpet vine, these characters tell a little story.*

Canaries (pages 30 and 31) 30½" x 38" (finished size)

Materials

- Muslin background and backing: 2⅓ yard
- Dark red border: ½ yard
- Dark green binding: ¼ yard
- Selection of colors for Appliqué
- Matching thread
- Quilting thread in natural color
- Floss: yellow, dark green, beige, white, dark gray, peach, brown
- Batting: 34" x 42"

Cutting

Cut muslin background 28" x 36". Trim to 25½" x 33" after appliqué and embroidery are complete.

Dark red border: cut four strips 3" wide selvage to selvage. Measure for exact length before you stitch. See Borders page 14.

Dark green binding: cut four strips 2" wide selvage to selvage. Measure for exact length before you stitch. See Binding page 15.

Lay out your design on paper creating the tree first. Place the cat, then the goldfinches. Add the tree leaves, vine, vine leaves, and lastly, the trumpet vine flowers. Note the two lower birds are Bird A, one as is and one reversed, and the upper bird is Bird B. See individual bird patterns. Transfer your paper design to the muslin background.

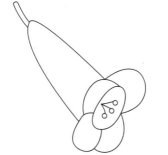

Appliqué

Stitch the branches first; the smaller branches, then the larger, noting the ones that are in front of others. Appliqué the tree trunk, leaving the edges unstitched where the vine stems will slide under. Appliqué the vine stems using bias (see pages 11), leaving free the one that will be over the cat.

The cat: Appliqué the body first, following the appliqué order. Pre-appliqué 16, 17, 18 and sew the back ear to the background. Appliqué 19. Pre-appliqué 20, 21, and 22. Note the pink ear lining is behind, using reverse appliqué, but you can sew it on top of 22 if you wish. Sew the completed forward ear to the background. Continue sewing in order. Pre-appliqué the eye in the order given on the pattern and appliqué as a whole. Pre-appliqué the muzzle sides to a piece of black and attach the unit (31) to the cat. Last, add the pink nose (32).

When the cat is complete, sew down the spaces in the trunk over the vine and the vine stem that goes over the cat. Appliqué all the leaves. Add the flowers and buds following the appliqué order given. Add goldfinches referring to the individual bird patterns for appliqué order.

Embroidery

Follow the individual bird patterns for the embroidery for the goldfinches. Adjust the feet and legs to fit the branches. Use a dark green double row of stem stitch for the flower and bud stems. Use two rows of brown stem stitch for the tree leaf stems. Put three short radiating single stitches in yellow out of the flower centers.

Use a beige stem stitch for the cat's eyebrows and whiskers. Run a black line of stem stitch along the bottom edge of the eye. Use white stitches to make a small white dot in the cat's eye.

Remove any markings and press. Trim to 25½" x 33" and add border. Press and baste for quilting.

Quilting

Cut a five-inch circle from a non-raveling fabric such as non-woven interfacing. (I used a piece of boiled wool.) Starting at the lower right corner, pin down the circle and quilt around the edge. Keep moving the circle and stitching around it. I did maneuver to cause a circle to encompass the top of each bird and the cat's head. Avoid an entire circle anywhere. Run the quilting design right through the border but not over the appliqué. After you have covered the entire piece with overlapping circles, quilt ¼" inside each circle's curved edge. I alternated filling the circles with random shells and ½" cross-hatching except for each bird and the cat's head. Here I made upwardly radiating lines. See photo for reference.

Check the size and trim the quilt to the top's edge, keeping it square. Remove the basting and bind.

See template on pattern page

Five in the Forest

A woodland world of maple and cherry in fruit is filled with life. The Red-Headed Woodpecker (page 48) climbs the trunk, the Chickadee (page 27), Nuthatch (page 39) and Wren (page 49) hide among the leaves as a Cliff Swallow (page 43) soars past for a look. This type of design is infinitely changeable using a variety of trees and birds.

Five in the Forest 26" x 36" (finished size)

Materials

- Muslin background and backing: 2 yards
- Red border: ⅓ yard
- Black binding: ¼ yard
- Selection of colors for Appliqué
- Matching thread
- Quilting thread in natural color
- Floss: green, gray, black, white, brown, tan
- Batting: 29" x 39"

Cutting

Cut muslin background 25" x 34", trim to 23" x 32" after appliqué and embroidery are complete.

Red border: cut four strips 2½" wide selvage to selvage. Measure for exact length before you stitch. See Borders page 14.

Black binding: cut four strips 2" wide selvage to selvage. Measure for exact length before you stitch. See Binding page 15.

Design your branches and trunk. See Designing page 15. Add leaves, berries and, finally, birds. There is a lot of room for change in this pattern. You may add or subtract as much as you like.

Appliqué

Start with branches, beginning with the smaller ones and moving to the larger. Note which is behind the other and appliqué accordingly. Leave free the branch that crosses the Chickadee as well as the one that crosses the Swallow. Appliqué these after the birds are complete. Add the leaves, cherries and seeds. Pre-appliqué the two-piece cherry leaves. *Slow and steady on the maple leaves.* See Inside Curves page 11. Note the order of appliqué for the maple seeds on the pattern. See Circles page 12 to aid in the appliqué of the cherries. See individual bird patterns for appliqué order.

Embroidery

Use two lines of green stem stitch for the leaf stems and main cherry stems, as well as the maple seed stems. Use one line of green stem stitch to attach the cherries to the main stem. Refer to the individual bird patterns for embroidery instruction.

Remove any markings and press. Trim to 23" x 32" and add borders. Press and baste for quilting.

Quilting

Begin with four scattered medium-size feathers. Add the sunlight lines radiating from top to bottom at a slight angle. Run double lines of quilting like branches ¼" apart, cutting the area into sections. Fill some of the resulting sections with radiating lines in various directions. Fill a lesser number of sections with random seed shapes. Continue the quilting into the borders, but not into the tree trunk or other appliqué. See photo for reference.

Trim the piece to the top's edge. Remove the basting and bind.

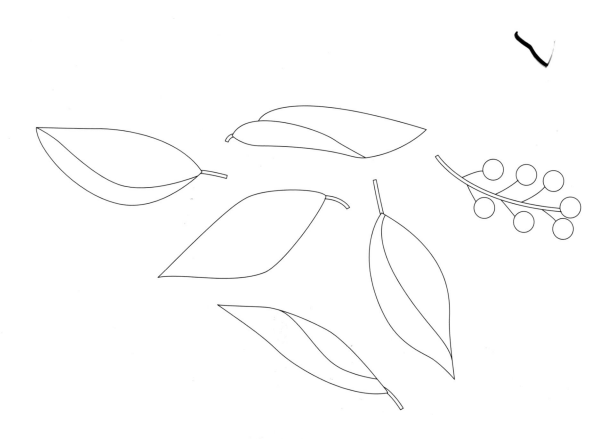

Feathered Stars

A *static design with six birds highlighted in a quilted eight-point star. This design can be made larger to accommodate more birds or pared down for only a few.*

The birds are each in an appropriate habitat: Baltimore Oriole (page 40) with elderberry, Scarlet Tanager (page 44) on a crab apple branch, Evening Grosbeak (page 32) amid fruiting box elder, Meadowlark (page 38) in seeded grass and the Rose-Breasted Grosbeak (page 33) among the blowing autumn leaves showing off his rose underwings in flight. Lastly the Cedar Waxwing (page 47) enjoys a meal in the pyrocantha.

Feathered Stars 28" x 41½" (finished size)

Materials

- Muslin background and backing: 2½ yards

- Black binding: ¼ yard

- Selection of colors for Appliqué

- Matching thread

- Quilting thread in natural color

- Floss: black, greens, brown, white, gray (refer to the individual bird patterns for additional colors)

- Batting: 34" x 48"

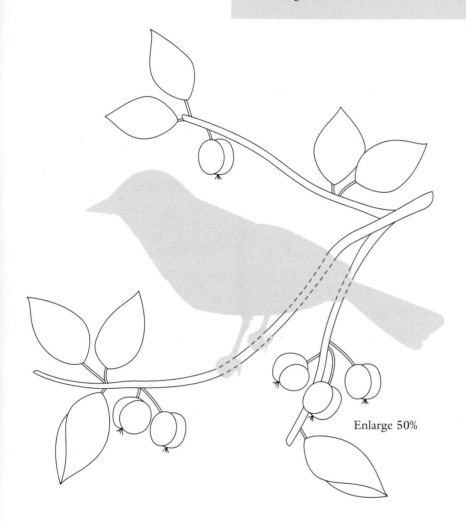

Enlarge 50%

Cutting

Cut muslin background
33" x 47"

Black binding: cut four strips 2"
wide selvage to selvage. Measure for
exact length before you stitch. See
Binding page 15.

Cut a piece of paper 14" square.
Fold in half, and in half again
lengthwise. Open and repeat in the
opposite direction. You now have a
grid. With a pencil and ruler, using
the diagram below as a reference,
mark the star block pattern. (Refer to full-size
template on pattern sheet.) Create your bird
designs roughly within the star area. Create as
many blocks as you wish.

Mark a 14" grid on the background material. Mark
the corners only, using a light color thread and a few
quick stitches. This mark can be ironed. See diagram.

Using a lightbox, trace your bird designs for appliqué as
usual on the background fabric. The thread corner marks
will be your guide in placement.

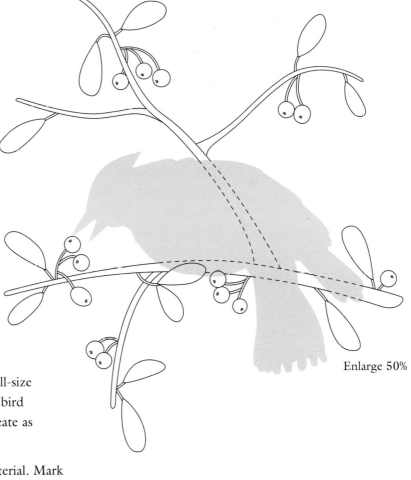

Enlarge 50%

With a pencil and ruler, using the
diagram below as a reference or the
full-size template (on perforated
pattern), mark the star block pattern.

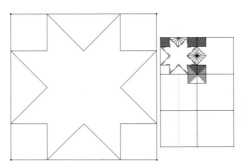

See template on
pattern page

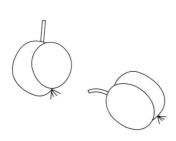

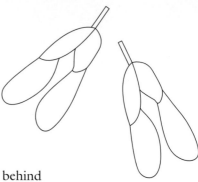

Appliqué

Appliqué the background stems, etc., that are behind the birds. Note the smaller branches are appliquéd first. Add leaves and berries. Refer to the detail for appliqué order where needed. See the individual bird patterns for their appliqué order. Finish with berries or leaves that are in front of any birds.

Enlarge 50%

Embroidery

Use the individual bird patterns for embroidery directions. Use stem stitch for leaf, berry and other stems. Add French knots to berries, and add small single stitches to the crab apples.

Remove any markings and press. Before basting, lightly mark all the straight lines between dots. Using your original pattern and the lightbox, mark the star outline using the thread dots to line up the piece on the pattern. Baste for quilting.

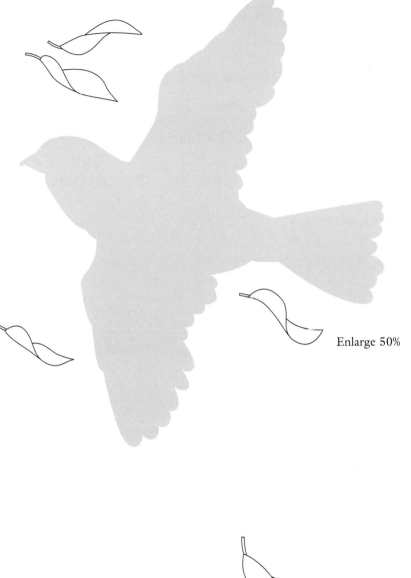

Enlarge 50%

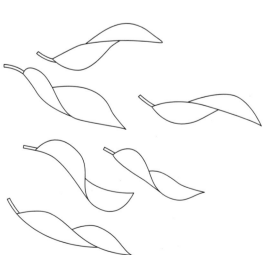

Enlarge 50%

Quilting

Quilt the straight lines between the thread dots first and then the star outline. Quilt 1/4" inside the star outline. You can eye this or use 1/4" masking tape. Quilt around each bird closely and then 1/4" out. Stitch random shells outward from the bird but keep this design within the star. Crosshatch with 3/4" spaces on the diagonal in each square formed at the block corners. Radiate lines in on-point at sides, top and bottom of blocks.

Quilt 1/4" around the entire outside quilt line. Refer to diagram below for reference (and on perforated page) for quilting. See photo for reference.

Trim the quilt 1/2" outside from the last quilted line. Using the last quilting line as a guide, sew on the binding. You may find it easier to stitch from the back where the quilting is visible. See Binding page 15.

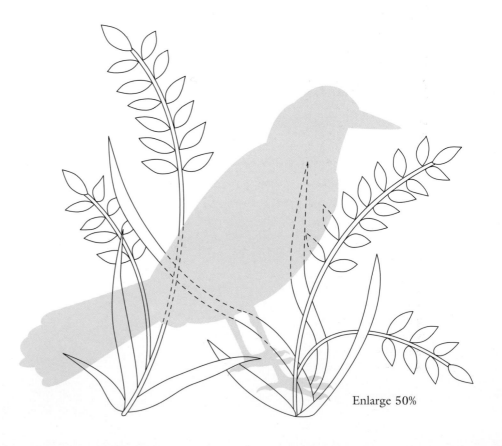

Enlarge 50%

About the Author

Carol Armstrong taught herself to quilt in 1980, developing her unique and highly artistic style. She uses her favorite technique, "Lightbox Appliqué." Botanically correct conventionalized celebrations of flora and birds are her strongest output, though any subject that catches her artistic eye may end up a minutely detailed grace on fabric.

In 1986 Carol moved to Michigan's Upper Peninsula, where she lives with her cabinetmaker husband, J.M. Friedrich, in the country near Shingleton. Carol says the wonderfully snowy winters give her time to do lots of quilting while her husband "Red" makes fine craft items in his workshop a path away. When her fingers and eyes need a diversion, there is always water to pump and bring in the house, wood to load into the woodbox, bird feeders to fill, or the large organic vegetable garden to tend.

Bibliography

Armstrong, Carol. Wildflowers. Lafayette, CA: C&T Publishing, Inc., 1998

Sew beautiful wildflower gardens using Carol Armstrong's original appliqué patterns. Nature springs to life in quilts, wallhangings, and home decorations as you mix and match twenty-four wildflower patterns to create your own version of the great outdoors.

Instructions are provided for ten projects, with explanations of Carol's methods for lightbox appliqué, pre-appliqué, and the needle-turn stitch. Also included are Carol's innovative techniques for free-form quilting designs that simulate rain, wind, sunlight, rocks, leaves, and other elements found in our natural world. Delicate watercolor illustrations throughout the book highlight the individual flowers.

For quilting supplies:
Cotton Patch Mail Order
3405 Hall Lane, Dept. CTB
Lafayette, CA 94549
e-mail: quiltusa@yahoo.com
web: www.quiltusa.com
(800) 835-4418
(925) 283-7883

Index

Other Fine Books From C&T

Appliqué 12 Easy Ways! : Charming Quilts, Giftable Projects & Timeless Techniques, Elly Sienkiewicz
Art & Inspirations: Ruth B. McDowell, Ruth B. McDowell
At Home with Patrick Lose: Colorful Quilted Projects, Patrick Lose
The Best of Baltimore Beauties, Elly Sienkiewicz
Beyond the Horizon: Small Landscape Appliqué, Valerie Hearder
Elegant Stitches: An Illustrated Stitch Guide & Source Book of Inspiration, Judith Baker Montano
Everything Flowers: Quilts from the Garden, Jean and Valori Wells
Faces & Places: Images in Appliqué, Charlotte Warr Andersen
Fancy Appliqué: 12 Lessons to Enhance Your Skills, Elly Sienkiewicz
Focus on Features: Life-like Portrayals in Appliqué, Charlotte Warr Andersen
Free Stuff for Stitchers on the Internet, Judy Heim and Gloria Hansen
Hand Quilting with Alex Anderson: Six Projects for Hand Quilters, Alex Anderson
Jacobean Rhapsodies: Composing with 28 Appliqué Designs, Patricia B. Campbell and Mimi Ayars
Mastering Quilt Marking: Marking Tools & Techniques, Choosing Stencils, Matching Borders & Corners, Pepper Cory

On the Surface: Thread Embellishment & Fabric Manipulation, Wendy Hill
Quilts from Europe, Projects and Inspiration, Gül Laporte
Quilts from the Civil War: Nine Projects, Historical Notes, Diary Entries, Barbara Brackman
Rx for Quilters: Stitcher-Friendly Advice for Every Body, Susan Delaney Mech, M.D.
Skydyes: A Visual Guide to Fabric Painting, Mickey Lawler
Special Delivery Quilts, Patrick Lose
Travels with Peaky and Spike: Doreen Speckmann's Quilting Adventures, Doreen Speckmann
Willowood: Further Adventures in Buttonhole Stitch Appliqué, Jean Wells
Women of Taste: A Collaboration Celebrating Quilt Artists and Chefs, Girls, Inc.

For more information write for a free catalog:
C&T Publishing, Inc.
P.O. Box 1456
Lafayette, CA 94549
(800) 284-1114
http://www.ctpub.com
e-mail: ctinfo@ctpub.com